THE NSTA READY-REFERENCE GUIDE TO

SAFER SCIENCE

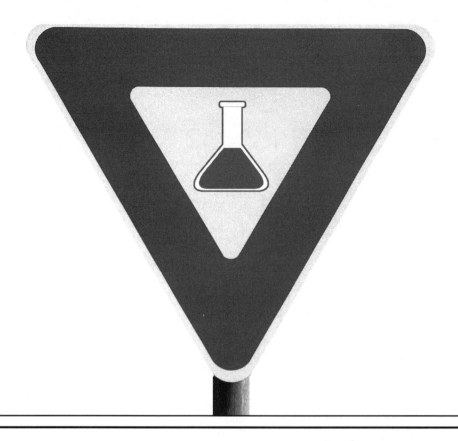

THE NSTA READY-REFERENCE GUIDE TO
SAFER
SCIENCE

An NSTA Press Journals Collection

KENNETH RUSSELL ROY

NATIONAL SCIENCE TEACHERS ASSOCIATION

Arlington, Virginia

Claire Reinburg, Director
Judy Cusick, Senior Editor
Andrew Cocke, Associate Editor
Betty Smith, Associate Editor
Robin Allan, Book Acquisitions Coordinator

SCIENCE SCOPE
Inez Luftig, Editor
Kenneth L. Roberts, Managing Editor
Janna Palliser, Associate Editor

ART AND DESIGN
Will Thomas, Jr., Director
Joseph Butera, Cover and Interior Design

PRINTING AND PRODUCTION
Catherine Lorrain, Director
Jack Parker, Electronic Prepress Technician

NATIONAL SCIENCE TEACHERS ASSOCIATION
Gerald F. Wheeler, Executive Director
David Beacom, Publisher

Library of Congress Cataloging-in-Publication Data

Roy, Kenneth Russell.
  The NSTA ready-reference guide to safer science / Kenneth Russell Roy.
     p. cm.
  Includes index.
  ISBN 978-1-933531-28-1
  1. Science--Experiments--Safety measures--Handbooks, manuals, etc. 2. Scientific apparatus and instruments-
-United States--Safety measures--Handbooks, manuals, etc. 3. Hazardous substances--United States--Safety
measures--Handbooks, manuals, etc. 4. Science--Study and teaching--United States. I. Title.
Q182.3.R69 2007
507.8--dc22

                                        2007034665

▽ CONTENTS

I. INTRODUCTION

II. SAFETY PRACTICES AND LEGAL STANDARDS

General Safety In Science

Chemical Safety

Physical Safety

Biological Safety

III. SAFETY IN SCIENCE INSTRUCTION

General Science

Chemical Science

Physical Science

Biological Science

IV. QUESTIONS FROM TEACHERS
General Questions

APPENDICES

▽ PREFACE

A s the French say, "Plus ca change, plus c'est la meme chose." "The more things change, the more they stay the same." This is the case with learning science in the classroom by "doing" hands-on activities. During the late 1950s and early 1960s after the Russian Sputnik started the space race, science education in the United States had a rebirth. The focus was placed on learning about science through the doing of science. A number of hands-on, process, and inquiry-based programs were developed with support from the National Science Foundation and other private groups and companies. Known as the "alphabet-soup" programs, they included SCIS (Science Curriculum Improvement Study), SAPA (Science A Process Approach), ESS (Earth Systems Science), IPS (Introductory Physical Science), and BSCS (Biological Sciences Curriculum Study). They were introduced and used in many schools throughout the United States at K–12 levels. Then, in the 1970s through the early 1990s, these programs fell out of favor for a variety of curricular, administrative, and financial reasons. And science teaching returned to the pre-1950s textbook, reading-about-science approach.

The mid-1990s brought the creation of the National Science Education Standards on the heels of the early 1980s A Nation At Risk followed by No Child Left Behind legislation after the turn of the century, and a number of curriculum programs including the American Association for the Advancement of Science Project 2061; the National Science Teacher Association's (NSTA) Scope, Sequence and Coordination; the State Science Frameworks; and more. Thus began the rebirth or return to the doing-of-science approach to science education.

Concurrently, during the early 1990s, the Occupational Safety and Health Administration (OSHA) unveiled and put into effect a new federal law covering laboratory safety, known as 29 CFR 1910.1450 "Occupational Exposure to Hazardous Chemicals in Laboratories" or the Laboratory Standard. This law put general industry employers, including school boards of education, on notice that they must provide for a safe workplace in laboratories to deal with hazardous chemicals and prudent practices.

In addition to OSHA's Laboratory Standard and the national education reports, a third factor that has influenced the direction of science education is the focus on a more diverse student population, including special-needs students. A series of legislative actions, including the Americans With Disabilities Act, required that all students have the opportunities to participate in general education, including science education. Laboratory design and construction, in addition to curriculum and instruction strategies, must attempt in earnest to address these needs.

The fourth factor is the revolution taking place in the cadre of science educators. As in the 1960s, a large group of science educators is reaching retirement age and leaving the profession. With them goes many years of professional experience and knowledge. New teachers with limited experience in laboratory work are taking their places.

The last important factor is liability. We are living in a litigious society in which teachers' actions are held to very high standards. Teachers and administrators need to become aware and concerned about liability. This is especially of interest to science teachers at the middle and high school levels, given the safety issues they face by working with students in formal laboratories and in fieldwork.

All of these factors have science teachers asking how they can improve safety in their laboratories and still carry out meaningful activities.

In order to meet some of these challenges, NSTA decided to introduce the column "Scope on Safety" for middle and junior high school science teachers in its middle school journal *Science Scope*. The purpose of the column is simple—provide safety information for middle grade science teachers to help them in addressing the safety issues of hands-on instruction in the laboratory and in the field.

This book is a compendium of those articles starting from the column's inception in February 2003. The articles are based on inquiries from school science teachers nationwide. The topics focus on everyday safety issues that middle grade science teachers and supervisors have to deal with in the doing of science. Each column is written to help the science teacher become aware of legal standards and prudent practices that help make for safe laboratory experiences and also protect both students and teachers. Unfortunately, some architects, building contractors, school administrators, and boards of education members have taken advantage of science teachers on issues such as facility design, occupancy loads, protective equipment, and more. This has happened because science teachers lack the expertise—knowledge and experience—in legal building and safety standards and prudent practices in the laboratory. Unsafe laboratory activities and unsafe laboratory facilities can get science teachers into legal challenges with professional and civil consequences.

The book is divided into four areas. The first is a short introduction to the topics of hands-on science for all students and also protection afforded the science teacher with the introduction of the OSHA Laboratory Standard. The second section addresses safety practices and legal standards with focus on current issues facing science teachers. The third section deals with safety in science instruction. It provides specific information on how to best incorporate safety in various aspects of science teaching. The final section answers questions middle grades teachers asked, through the column, about everyday issues.

Building safe science behaviors begins at the elementary and middle school levels. These practices serve as the guidelines to future laboratory work with many carryovers into everyday life. Safe science is critical for the teacher as an instructor and employee and for the student as a learner and citizen. Learning to teach and practice safe science is a lifelong endeavor, and I hope you will join me in it.

Ken Roy

▽ ACKNOWLEDGMENTS

Special thanks to Ken Roberts, *Science Scope* managing editor, and Inez Fugate Liftig, field editor, for their guidance and direction in the development and operation of the column over the years. Thanks also go to David Beacom, publisher, for his ongoing support and action relative to addressing safety issues in NSTA publications. I could not successfully continue my safety crusade without the love and encouragement from my wife Marisa, my daughters Louise Roy and Lisa Motyl, and my grandson Michael Bride.

▽ ABOUT THE AUTHOR

Kenneth Russell Roy has been a science teacher and administrator for more than 39 years. In addition, he has a large number of experiences as an author and editor with more than 150 published articles and four books dealing with science education and laboratory safety. He has served in numerous leadership positions for state, national, and international science education organizations. He currently serves as the Director of Environmental Health and Safety for Glastonbury Public Schools, Glastonbury, Connecticut. Roy is also an independent safety consultant/adviser working with professional organizations, school districts, magnet schools, insurance companies, textbook publishers, and other organizations dealing with safety issues.

He earned a bachelor's in science in 1968 and a master's in 1974 from Central Connecticut State University and a PhD in 1985 from the University of Connecticut. In addition, he received a Diploma in Professional Education from the University of Connecticut in 1981 and has a Certificate of Instruction as an Authorized OSHA Instructor from the Keene State College OSHA (Office of Safety and Health Administration) Extension School.

Roy is past chairperson of the NSTA Science Safety Advisory Board and is now NSTA Science Safety Consultant, serving as NSTA liaison to the board.

▽ ABOUT THIS BOOK

Beginning in February 2003, *Science Scope* started publishing the column "Scope on Safety," in each issue. In the column, author Ken Roy, NSTA Science Safety Consultant and past chairperson of the NSTA Safety Advisory Board, shares the knowledge, skills, and attitudes that help guide safety planning. The book includes information, anecdotes, advisories, and warnings, and good leads to the newest resources, and it answers questions on safety from teachers.

This guide is a compilation of all the columns through summer of 2007 in quick-reference form, and it covers a wide range of safety issues. You can use the index or the table of contents to find the right page for quick answers to your questions on practicing safer science.

"Relativity" isn't just science. It sometimes guides your judgments in science education too. Every day, in every lesson, science teachers make decisions about safety relative to the maturity and knowledge base of their students and the environment in which they teach.

Science safety isn't just a set of rules. It requires common sense and that teacher intuition that helps predict what might happen when we least expect it. To foster inquiry in a safe environment, teachers must not only keep up-to-date with the latest information about products, hazards, and best practice but also consider the developmental level of their budding scientists.

As always, remember that the best piece of safety equipment in your classroom is you—the informed adult shaping and controlling the learning environment.

SECTION

I

INTRODUCTION

▽ Safety Is for Everyone

The 1996 National Research Council's *National Science Education Standards* reflects a strong commitment to science education for all students. The Standards reject any situation in which some people are discouraged from pursuing science and excluded from opportunities to learn it. In concert with the Standards, federal laws and regulations mandate equal access and inclusion to the maximum extent possible in the general education curriculum for all students. Two key pieces of legislation include Public Law 94-142 (Education for All Handicapped Children Act), and Public Law 105-17 (The Individuals With Disabilities Education Act—IDEA).

Other federal and state general industry standards for science laboratory safety have been evolving. The regulations began in 1986 with the advent of the Occupational Safety and Health Administration's (OSHA) 29 CFR 1910.1200 (Hazard Communication Standard). It was followed up in 1990 with 29 CFR 1910.1450 (Occupational Exposure to Hazardous Chemicals in Laboratories Standard).

In some ways, the laboratory safety standards may seem to be at odds with science laboratory curriculum expectations in an environment attempting to provide for full inclusion of all students. Clearly, not all students will be able to be fully mainstreamed and may require alternative placement. Careful planning and appropriate accommodations in terms of instructional strategies and assistive technology, however, can provide for equitable access to hands-on science education for all students in a safe learning environment.

Raising the Bar

The challenge for science teachers is to meet the needs of each of their students while maintaining high standards and attempting to raise the educational bar. It is important that special-needs students not be singled out in the classroom. Also, in a team teaching situation (a science teacher teaming with a special education teacher), each teacher must be responsible for all students in the classroom. The science teacher ensures the meeting of curriculum goals, and the special education teacher works to modify and adapt the instructional approaches to those students having IEPs (individual education plans). Although there may be some unique challenges in working with mainstreamed or self-contained students with special-needs in a laboratory situation, teachers should consider alternatives or modifications for providing a safe and effective experience that addresses both special education laws and safety regulation standards.

Special Needs and Safety

For the science teacher, several website resources may prove to be useful. West Virginia University has a website (*www.as.wvu.edu/~scidis*) for teaching science to students with disabilities, which includes lists of teaching strategies by disability. Do-It at the University of Washington in Seattle (*www.washington.edu/doit*) offers workshops, links, and strategies for students and teachers in science. The Parents and Educators Resource Center (*www.schwablearning.org*) offers the Assistive Technology Guide.

In an effort to better meet the science laboratory safety needs for all students, the following strategies are suggested:

- Modify a laboratory activity,

- Secure specialized lab safety and instructional equipment,

- Improve your knowledge level of special needs,

- Eliminate a laboratory activity, or

- Provide an alternative activity for the special-needs student.

Lab safety considerations

- Plan and practice for a barrier-free egress in case of laboratory evacuation.

- Use only plastic or safety glass on all doors or windows in the laboratory.

- Make laboratory doorways wide enough to accommodate wheelchairs or students on crutches.

- Meet minimum net square footage for occupancy loads in consideration of strategically arranged furniture for appropriately sized aisles and numbers of exit doors.

- Provide appropriate safety and instructional equipment including low-profile eyewash/shower, lab station, and reduced height chalk and marker boards.

- Modify utility controls to allow for access to water, gas, and electricity.

- Install computer wires and other cables in a way to prevent tripping hazards.

Instruction safety considerations

- Have special-needs student work with a nonhandicapped student willing to serve in a partner situation or, if necessary, a special education aide.

- Except for modification predetermined by an IEP or PPT (planning and placement team), use consistency in assessment and behavioral expectations of all students.

Although special-needs students often have unique skills or assistive technology to compensate, some activities may need modification. Use a variety of instructional methodologies to compensate for visual and auditory needs

Middle school science teachers can use the "AAA" approach to safety in dealing with special-needs students: Have *awareness* of special-needs students, do an *assessment* for appropriate safety precautions, and take *action* to ensure safety and learning for all students in the science laboratory.

Reference

National Research Council (NRC). 1996. *National Science Education Standards*. Washington, DC: National Academy Press.

▽ BUILD IN SAFETY: OSHA LABORATORY STANDARD

Start With a Strong Foundation

How often have science teachers heard these statements?

- We just don't have enough money in the budget for eyewash stations in your science rooms. Besides, your classrooms are not real science laboratories—don't worry about it!

- I wouldn't be concerned about the ventilation in your laboratory. Smell is part of the territory.

- I don't care if you think that science laboratory was built for 24 students. If I want to put 35 students in there, I will—and you will teach them.

Unfortunately, these types of statements are being made with increased frequency by principals, superintendents, boards of education members, and other decision makers.

Their attitude creates a major stumbling block for science educators in terms of curriculum and instruction and liability. On one hand, teachers are being asked to provide more hands-on activity based science as supported by the National Science Education Standards, with additional impetus coming from the No Child Left Behind legislation and state-level frameworks. On the other hand, they are being told that class size and funding for texts and other support materials are in jeopardy because of increasing enrollments, outdated or inadequate facilities, and declining fiscal support.

The fact is that doing science in a laboratory costs more money and takes more time than reading about science in a classroom. If we are to improve science education by moving in the directions advocated by national reform movements, science educators must take a greater role in helping decision makers better understand and support these initiatives.

One major area that needs to be targeted is laboratory safety. It is one thing to advocate the doing of science. It is a whole other thing to provide a safer laboratory in which these activities take place. To this end, it is critical for science teachers and administrators to become knowledgeable about safety codes and laws. They must be advocates, working with decision makers and helping support them in keeping science laboratories safe for employees and students.

Providing a safe working environment for teachers and students is a serious responsibility for school districts as employers. The foundations for laboratory safety are the Occupational Safety and Health Administration's (OSHA) Occupational Exposure to Hazardous Chemicals in Laboratories or the "Laboratory Standard" for employees working in laboratories, including academic laboratories such as those found in middle schools. OSHA defines the term *laboratory* as "a facility where the laboratory use of hazardous chemicals occurs. It is a workplace where relatively small quantities of hazardous chemicals are used on a non-production basis."

Most public employers under federal OSHA or State Plan OSHA are required to cover laboratory workers (including science teachers) with the Laboratory Standard, 29 CFR 1910.1450 Subpart Z. Science teachers should secure information on which health and safety standards protect them on the job site in their state.

Frame a Strong Safety Program

A strong safety program must to be framed in the design of OSHA's Laboratory Standard. This standard is performance based, meaning that OSHA outlines the basic requirements and then each employer writes a plan tailored to its needs. For example, plans on specific procedures for securing chemicals may vary from district to district, but all plans must contain procedures for purchasing chemicals. The standard also requires that the employer (e.g., board of education) appoint a chemical hygiene officer (CHO) to develop and implement a chemical hygiene plan (CHP).

The basic framework that must be included in the CHP includes the following:

- Scope and Application—This standard covers any employee who is engaged in the laboratory use of hazardous chemicals on a laboratory scale (as opposed to industrial level). Science teachers as employees in middle school are classified under this application if they have a formal laboratory.

- Definitions—This section defines terms such as *action level, employee, laboratory, hazardous chemical,* and *chemical hygiene officer.* These terms are critical points of reference in writing the CHP and standard operating procedures.

- Permissible Exposure Limits (PELs)—Employees are not to be exposed above the permissible exposure limits specified in OSHA's 29 CFR 1910, Subpart Z.

- Employee Exposure Determination—This component requires employees' measurement of exposure to certain chemicals, such as mercury, if the action level or PEL is exceeded, providing a monitoring standard has been established. If monitoring is required, the employee must be notified of the results.

- Chemical Hygiene Plan (CHP) —A written plan must be developed to protect employees from hazards associated with chemicals in the laboratory.

- Employee Information and Training—Employees must be made aware of chemical hazards in the laboratory. The training must be provided at time of initial employment and when new chemicals or hazards are introduced into the workplace. Information must include CHP contents and the Laboratory Standard, PELs and threshold limit values (which define the reasonable level of a chemical substance to which a worker can be exposed with out adverse health effects), exposure signs, and location of related reference material. Training must minimally include methods to detect presence of hazardous chemicals, physical and chemical health hazards in the laboratory and work area, procedures including emergency procedures, work practices, and protective equipment.

- Medical Consultation and Medical Examination—Employer must provide an opportunity for employee medical support and follow-up examinations.

- Hazard Identification—A labeling system such as the National Fire Protection Association labeling codes must be adopted, and material safety data sheets (MSDSs) must be maintained and made available.

- Use of Respirators—When respirators are required as per 29 CFR 1910.134, procedure and equipment must be provided by the employer. In a middle school science lab, the activities should not warrant the need for respirators.

- Recordkeeping—Employers must keep records of exposure monitoring, medical consultation, and examinations of employees.

- Dates—CHP must have been developed and implemented by 31 January 1991.

- Appendices—Nonmandatory recommendations are provided for consideration in the CHP. Although the noted references are not endorsed by OSHA, they address professional expectations and provide specific safety protocols in the laboratory situation. A CHP will be more effective if based on these safety protocols.

Designing the Chemical Hygiene Plan

The CHP components are prescribed by the Laboratory Standard. Each plan must contain the following minimum parts:

1. Operating standards for laboratory operation, which all employees are required to follow.
2. Criteria to determine and implement control measures to reduce employee exposure, such as type of engineering controls (ventilation), use of personal protective equipment (PPE) (goggles), and hygiene practices (hand washing).
3. Requirement that fume hoods and other protective equipment are functioning properly and within specific measures.
4. Provisions for employee information and training, such as frequency and type of safety training and information.
5. Protocols in which laboratory operation requires prior approval from the employer.
6. Provisions for medical consultation and examinations if an employee has a chemical exposure or incident.
7. Designation of personnel responsible for implementation of CHP including achemical hygiene officer (CHO).
8. Provision for additional employee protection when working with particularly hazardous substances such as acid vapors.

These components represent the basic framework for the chemical hygiene plan. Additional items, such as occupancy load and security, can be addressed.

House of Safety

The OSHA Laboratory Standard is the foundation for building an effective laboratory safety program, but safety must be further developed as an ongoing attitude and commitment that never takes a rest. Science teachers and leadership must be advocates for safer science in the laboratory or field. They must work to help educate others to promote and facilitate a safer working environment for employees and students. Hands-on, process, and inquiry science can be fun and a great learning experience for students when designed and built with safety in mind.

References

Occupational Safety and Health Administration. 1990. Laboratories [Online]. Available at *www.osha-slc.gov/SLTC/laboratories/index.html* [1999, June 17] and *www.osha.gov/pls/oshaweb/owadisp.show_document?p_table=standards&p_id=10106*

SECTION

II

SAFETY PRACTICES AND LEGAL STANDARDS

▽ GENERAL SAFETY IN SCIENCE

1. About Asbestos

Asbestos has been used in the construction of elementary, middle, and high school ceilings, floor tile adhesives, pipe and structural beam insulations, science laboratory benches, wire gauss on ring stands, fume hood panels, general insulation, and more during the 1950s through early 1970s. Why? Primarily, asbestos was selected because of its fireproofing, acoustical, and sometimes decorative character.

Over time, as the asbestos-laden material began to dry, it became friable. In other words, it flakes off and becomes an airborne fine dust that suspends in school classrooms and laboratories.

In 1973, the U.S. Environmental Protection Agency (EPA) banned the use of spray-on asbestos materials because of a concern for potential long-term effects in children and teachers. Levels of airborne asbestos inside school buildings with asbestos-containing materials can exceed outdoor ambient levels by a factor of over 1,000.

In 1980, the EPA did a quantitative risk estimate for asbestos-containing materials in U.S. schools. The following estimated results were provided:

- More than 8,500 schools had friable asbestos.

- Approximately 3,000,000 students were potentially exposed.

- Approximately 250,000 teachers and other school employees were potentially exposed.

- Approximately 7,000 premature deaths are anticipated because of the exposure to prevalent concentrations of asbestos in schools with friable asbestos over the next 30 years. Ninety percent of these are expected to be exposed schoolchildren.

AHERA—Emergency Response

The EPA developed a series of additional legislative initiatives through the 1980s to help better protect students and school employees from asbestos. In 1986, the Asbestos Hazard Emergency Response Act (AHERA) became law. This legislation requires public and private nonprofit schools to inspect their buildings for asbestos-containing building materials. The EPA developed the following regulations that require schools subject to AHERA to

- Perform an original inspection and periodic re-inspections for asbestos-containing material every three years.

- Develop, maintain, and update an asbestos management plan and keep a copy at the school.

- Provide yearly notification to parent, teacher, and employee organizations regarding the availability of the school's asbestos management plan and any asbestos abatement actions taken or planned in the school.

- Designate a contact person to ensure the responsibilities of the local education agency are properly implemented.

- Perform periodic surveillance of known or suspected asbestos-containing building material.

- Provide custodial staff with asbestos awareness training.

Health Effects

Exposure to airborne friable asbestos can result in a potential health risk resulting from breathing in asbestos fibers. Fibers embedded in lung tissue over time can cause serious lung diseases including asbestosis, lung cancer, or mesothelioma. The list includes

- *Asbestosis*—This is a very serious long-term disease of the lungs caused by inhaling asbestos fibers and scarring of tissue. The scarring makes it difficult to breathe, causing shortness of breath. There is no treatment.

- *Lung cancer*—Lung cancer causes the largest number of deaths related to asbestos exposure. Common symptoms include coughing and a change in breathing. Other symptoms include shortness of breath, persistent chest pains, hoarseness, and anemia.

- *Mesothelioma*—This is a rare form of cancer found in the thin lining of the lung, chest, abdomen, and heart. It does not show up until many years of exposure to asbestos.

Dealing With Asbestos

Friable asbestos hazards are dealt with in four ways, depending on a number of factors such as location, size, cost, and so on. Acceptable remediation includes:

- Complete removal—remediation carried out under acceptable occupational guidelines. This process eliminates the asbestos source.

- Encapsulation—covering friable asbestos with sealants to prevent release of fibers.

- Enclosure—construction of airtight wall and ceilings adjacent to surface with friable asbestos. This approach will reduce exposure outside of the enclosed area.

- Periodic maintenance—inspection program needs to be set up to determine appreciable changes in cases where asbestos represents no immediate problems.

Finding Asbestos

Asbestos can still be found in school science laboratories, as well as other building locations. It is a matter of knowing where to look. The first thing is to ask for the AHERA asbestos management plan report required of all schools and updated every three years. This plan will provide infor-

mation about areas in the school known to have asbestos and actions taken to reduce or eliminate exposure. Science laboratories are special in that there are a variety of locations in which asbestos can be found. These areas, which include the following, should be investigated:

- Floor tile
- Insulated materials for pipes and structural beams
- Adhesive behind bulletin boards
- Black science counter and workbench tops
- Wire mesh pad with white material—for ring stand
- Large magnets insulated with fibrous materials
- Incubators
- Fume hood panels
- Sample of asbestos mineral (Earth/space science inventory)
- Vermiculite potting soil and insulation material

All schools have an annual requirement to notify parent-teacher groups about the availability of asbestos-removal plans that have been scheduled. Any school employee also has a right to review the plan. If there is concern about asbestos, the EPA regional asbestos coordinator can be informed.

Online Resource

U.S. Environmental Protection Agency (EPA) website—*www.epa.gov*. Click, near the top of the page, on the "Quick Finder" word *asbestos* for information.

2. Tracking Chemicals

A new middle school science teacher was interested in how chemicals were being tracked in his new school's science department. In helping to answer the new recruit's questions, the retiring science teacher gave him a tour of the chemical storeroom. The new teacher noticed that all of the chemicals were alphabetically arranged. "Why is that?" he asked. The retiring teacher noted he found it easy to locate chemicals using this system. Not seeing any dates on the bottles, the new teacher asked how old the chemicals were. "I have it all in my head," the retiring teacher said. He went on to say that other chemicals were stored in various parts of the building in laboratories and classrooms. Unfortunately, the retiring teacher had not gotten around to creating an inventory of chemicals on hand. The new teacher thanked the retiring teacher for the information and began thinking of the number of changes he would need to make in order to track and store each chemical in a safe way.

Unfortunately, this scenario is all too common in middle schools. The haphazard storing and tracking of chemicals in the laboratory is a serious safety issue facing science teachers. To get control of your chemicals, I suggest that you implement a *chemical tracking system (CTS)*.

Using Chemicals

A CTS is a database of chemicals used in the laboratory. If implemented correctly, a CTS will reduce purchasing costs, eliminate overstocking, and reduce disposal costs. It will also allow you to respond more effectively to accidents, fires, and other hazardous situations.

Working with chemicals in the middle school science laboratory requires prudent management in purchasing, using, storing, and disposing. Teachers need to have knowledge of how chemicals are to be used and how they interact with other chemicals. Information can be secured by using chemical labels, material safety data sheets (MSDSs) and other available resources. Once you've decided which chemicals to purchase, tracking is the next critical step.

Security is another critical issue because school districts and teachers are being held liable for injuries and suffering via civil liability if chemicals are not stored or controlled correctly. A CTS also helps you monitor your supplies more closely and makes theft and tampering more apparent.

The end goal in storage and tracking inventory is simple—to reduce the cost, waste, and environmental impact associated with using chemicals. By tracking chemicals from date of purchase until disposal, you can easily determine how often or with what frequency chemicals are used and will need to be replaced. This saves precious purchasing dollars and reduces needless waste.

A major part of the tracking system is a viable and effective inventory process. The components of such a system include a centralized inventory storage location, a management system, and personnel in charge of the program. An exceptionally user-friendly inventory system for CTS is available from vendors such as Flinn and the American Chemical Society (see Resources). If funding is limited, you can create your own inventory system using word processing or database software. A third alternative is a card filing system.

Steps to CTS

The following are components of an effective CTS:

Know what's in the container—Make sure chemicals are properly labeled. Purchased chemicals from credible suppliers should have appropriate labels. Mislabeled and unidentified chemicals usually are the result of students or teachers trying to save leftover chemicals in a new container and not creating a proper label. Be sure to use a standard labeling system for chemicals and waste products. Also, use permanent and colorfast ink when creating labels to prevent fading.

Don't make storing chemicals a shell game—As soon as chemicals are spread throughout a building in various storage areas, chemical control can be lost. The most efficient and safest approach to chemical storage in all laboratory work, including middle school labs, is the concept of centralization. This approach allows for a more organized, accountable, and credible approach to tracking chemical inventory and storage.

The tenets of an effective CTS are:

1. Always update and check your inventory system prior to purchasing additional chemicals. This will prevent overstocking and aging of chemicals.

2. Records for chemical inventories should include the following:

   • Date of inventory

   • Date chemical received

   • Specific amount of each chemical

   • Name, formula, and grade of each chemical printed on the container's label

   • Chemical hazard of each item (material safety data sheet information and National Fire Protection Association hazard code)

   • Chemical abstract service (CAS) registry number

   • Source (supplier)

   • Container type

   • Hazard classification

   • Required storage conditions

   • Expiration date

   • Storage location of each chemical

   • Amount of chemical in the container

3. Make sure new chemicals are dated upon receipt. Expired chemicals should be removed and slated for disposal.

4. Check expiration dates when selecting chemicals, and use older stock first.

5. Inventory audits are critical to determine which chemicals are being used and which are not. If you don't use it, lose it.

6. Sort out and remove from the inventory human carcinogens, teratogens (capable of causing birth defects), reproductive toxins, and mutagens (genetic damage). Toxic materials (cyanide salts), radioactive materials, and explosive materials should also be removed. Foster items in the inventory that pose lesser hazards of corrosivity, reactivity, and toxicity.

Chemical Orienteering

Use and care of chemicals can be like a hunt in the wild; success can be met only by using a good tracking system. Once the system is set up, it will save the teacher time, money, accountability, and liability.

Internet Resources

American Chemical Society—*www.acs.org*

Chemical management information—*www.instantref.com/tox-chem.htm*

Flinn Scientific Company—*www.flinnsci.com/Sections/Safety/safety.asp*

National Fire Protection Association—*www.nfpa.org*

Searchable chemical database—*chemfinder.camsoft.com*

3. Indoor Air

According to the American Lung Association, indoor air is up to 70 times more polluted than outdoor air. This is critical in light of the fact most people spend 60 to 90% of their time indoors. *Medical Digest* has stated that medical research points to the fact most headaches are allergic reactions to dust. The National Air Pollution Central Administration estimates that more than 43 million tons of dust falls on the United States yearly. According to *Spray Technology and Marketing* magazine, a major source of indoor air pollutants is street dust, carried in on shoes and captured in carpeting. The list goes on and on.

Now, add to the dust and dirt scenario the exposures in a laboratory environment (such as hazardous chemical vapors, particulates, gases, and so on) and you have the potential for serious levels of exposure and illness. This is especially exacerbated by poor or inadequate ventilation systems, a lack of custodial support, and nonexistent or unenforced hygiene policies.

Dirt on the Books

In fiscal year 2004, the Occupational Safety and Health Administration (OSHA) issued more than 1,100 citations for violations of Subpart D in General Industry Standards, which includes housekeeping rules (29 CFR 1910.22 [a]). This standard makes the following statement: "All places of employment, passageways, storerooms, and service rooms shall be kept clean and orderly and in a sanitary condition." This includes cleanup and removal of dust and dirt, containment and cleanup of small spills, and proper storage or disposal of hazardous substance containers.

The other relevant OSHA standard for science teachers is the Occupational Exposures to Hazardous Chemicals in Laboratories (29 CFR Part 1910.1450), also known as the Laboratory Standard. The written Chemical Hygiene Plans must include work practices, procedures, and policies to ensure employees are protected in the workplace (laboratory). Included are housekeeping, maintenance, and inspections:

- Cleaning: Floors should be cleaned regularly.

- Inspections: Formal housekeeping and chemical hygiene inspections should be held at least quarterly for places with frequent personnel changes and semiannually for others.

- Maintenance: Eyewash stations should be activated for 5 to 10 minutes on a weekly basis. Emergency showers should be tested at least annually.

- Passageways: Stairways and hallways should not be used as storage areas.

The laboratory facility should have appropriate general ventilation with air intakes and exhausts located so as to avoid re-entrainment of contaminated air. Typically, 8 to 10 room air changes per hour provide adequate general ventilation for occupied laboratories in schools. Additional health and safety housekeeping standards and regulations can be found in local and state health departments, environmental protection agencies, and school district policies.

Good Housekeeping Procedures

The science department needs to have standard operating procedures in place (as part of the Chemical Hygiene Plan required by the OSHA Laboratory Standard) that deal with housekeeping, including handling of daily dust and dirt. Listed in the procedures should be expectations for custodial and maintenance support, laboratory occupant procedures for cleanup and general operation, and so on. For example, use of HEPA-type (high-efficiency particulate air filter) vacuum cleaners by custodial staff is a must, compared to conventional vacuum cleaners, to get the dust and dirt out of the labs. Inquire about a preventative maintenance program by the school maintenance department for HVAC filters to be changed at appropriate times of the year. This will help filter out dust and dirt during the operation of the laboratory. Laboratories should be cleaned each night by trained custodial staff. Students should have clear responsibilities for cleaning up at the end of every laboratory activity. Don't wait until the end of the day for the custodian to clean the whole day's worth of dirt. Remember, students are constantly moving in and out of the laboratory all day long, bringing in more dirt and dust on clothing and footwear.

In selecting cleaning materials, use those with reduced environmental impact and a lower risk profile relative to health and safety. Look for petrochemical-free and plant/mineral-derived types of cleaners. Petroleum-based detergents contain toxic impurities such as benzene and other chemicals that cause allergic reactions in lungs, eyes, skin, and sinuses. Solvent cleaners contribute to air pollution, skin irritations, and allergies. Ammonia multipurpose cleaners have vapors with fumes that are highly irritating to the eyes and nose; high concentrations attack the lung membranes.

The goal is to minimize the risk of allergens for laboratory occupants. For example, a simple disinfectant can be made by filling a spray bottle with a 5 to 10% solution of eucalyptus oil. If hand wipes are used, select those without alcohol or antibacterials. For hand washing, use simple soap and water.

High volume and/or concentrated chemical use should be avoided in favor of microchemistry. Less is more! Try to select common household materials to illustrate concepts rather than laboratory chemicals whenever possible. They are generally cheaper, safer, and easier to use and dispose of properly. Adopting microchemistry practices would dramatically reduce allergens, such as highly volatile organic compound vapors.

Warehousing is another contributor to the buildup of dust and dirt. Science teachers love to save things for use in future years. The dust and dirt settles on these items left on top of cabinets, on bookshelves, and elsewhere. Remember to clean these items at least once or twice a year. Keep them covered in plastic or stored in drawers.

Remember, keeping the laboratory clean is an ongoing activity. Make sure procedures are in place with help from support staff to keep things rolling relative to cleanliness.

4. Ergonomics

Is your job a pain in the neck, wrist, or back? If so, *ergonomics* may provide you with some relief. Ergonomics is the science of adapting workstations, tools, equipment, and working practices to be compatible with the individual worker and thus reduce the possibility of injury.

Lab-based science instruction requires teachers to perform many repetitive tasks, such as writing on the chalkboard, using a microscope, keyboarding, and pipetting, which can lead to aches and pains. Many common problems, however, can be avoided if you are aware of your work environment and avoid certain behaviors. The following are some of the more common ergonomic-related hazards of working in the lab and suggestions for avoiding them.

Carpal tunnel syndrome (CTS) and cumulative trauma disorder (CTD) are two task-related injuries. CTS is the result of repetitive hand and wrist motions. The median nerve that runs through the carpal tunnel can become swollen with repeated use. This causes pain and loss of sensation in the hand. CTD is the result of the overuse or improper use of a joint. For example, sitting at a poorly designed computer workstation can cause knee joint pain and damage to tendons, muscles, and nerves. To prevent CTS and CTD, teachers should

- minimize space between fingers to reduce stress on tendons;

- limit repetitive actions to a short period of time (an hour or less) and flex and shake hands during breaks;

- avoid using a two-finger pinch grip when performing actions such as pipetting—grasp objects with your entire hand instead; and

- use a wrist rest and keep wrists straight and forearms parallel to the surface when keyboarding.

Computer Eyestrain

Unless you are working at an ergonomically designed workstation, using a computer can result in eyestrain, neck aches, backaches, and headaches. Unfortunately, most teachers do their keyboarding at desks, on lab tables, and in other spaces that were not designed with computer use in mind. The Centers for Disease Control recommends that a computer workstation should

- include adjustable keyboard platforms that are installed under the lab tables—wireless keyboards provide the most ergonomic benefits;

- be positioned in corners or protected areas from artificial and natural light;

- include a monitor at eye level, adjusted to the proper brightness and contrast, with a viewing range of 45–76 cm (18–30 inches);

- provide a document holder next to the computer screen at the same height; and

- provide footrests to accommodate changes in leg positions.

Sittings at the station should be broken up with breaks about every 30 minutes.

Microscope Advice

If you will be spending a lot of time bent over a microscope, keep these recommendations in mind:

- Avoid long periods of microscope work (more than five hours per day). Uninterrupted periods of use should also be avoided.

- Try to keep an upright position or posture by placing the microscope near the edge of the workstation.

- Try to use an area that provides support for the forearms.

- Use an ergonomically designed chair

or stool with back support and adjustable height.

- Try to make use of footrests.

Lifting

Teachers spend a lot of time putting things in and taking things out of storage. When doing so, remember to

- use a stepladder, footstool, or other appropriate and stable means to secure objects above shoulder level;

- store heavy objects in cabinets or shelves below shoulder height;

- lift objects directly in front of you, and never twist while lifting; and

- lift with your knees, not your back muscles.

Remember that ergonomic-related problems often take months to years to surface. Science teachers and other school employees need to be proactive by addressing ergonomic issues before the damage is done.

Internet Resources

Centers for Disease Control and Prevention (CDC)—*www.cdc.gov/od/ohs/Ergonomics/labergo.htm*

National Institutes of Health (NIH)—*http://odp.od.nih.gov/whpp/ergonomics/laboratory.html*

5. Eye Protection

Science laboratory activities and classroom demonstrations can be both fun and serious. Fun in that the students get nature to expose a few of its secrets in interesting ways. Serious in that there needs to be respect for the equipment and materials used in experiments and demonstrations in order to stay out of harm's way. Laboratory accidents and near misses in schools are often caused by the lack of personal protective equipment, such as eye protection. Sophisticated acids and other corrosive chemicals are not the only substances that put eyes in jeopardy. A household item as simple as vinegar can cause damage if handled inappropriately. So, what are the rules, dangers, and protections required?

Most states have adopted general statutes relative to regulations concerning eye-protective devices in schools. For example, Connecticut's Statute section 10-214a-1 reads "any person who is working, teaching, observing, supervising, assisting in or engaging in any work, activity or study in a public or private elementary or secondary school laboratory or workshop where the process tends to damage the eyes or where protective devices can reduce the risk of injury to the eyes concomitant with such activity shall wear an eye protective device of industrial quality in the manner in which such device was intended to be worn." This includes science laboratories, technology education laboratories, art studios, and vocational and technical education facilities.

In addition to state legislation, the Occupational Safety and Health Administration (OSHA) requires employees to wear appropriate personal protective equipment for eye protection including safety spectacles/glasses or goggles (29 CFR 1910.133). Additional references are noted in areas such as the Hazard Communications/Right to Know standard (29 CFR 1910.1200) and the Occupational Exposure to Hazardous Chemicals in Laboratories/Laboratory Standard (29 CFR 1910.1450). The appropriate eye protection is dependent on the hazard the worker is, or can be, exposed to in the workplace.

Laboratory Dangers

Many sources of danger to the eyes create a need for eye protection in middle school science laboratories and classrooms. Some examples of sources and the necessary protective eye devices for science activities are

- acid or other corrosive chemicals (vinegar, ammonia, detergents, and solvents)—use chemical-splash proof goggles;

- dust producing operations (wood dust)—use chemical-splash goggles;

- hot liquids, solids, and gases (heating or boiling water)—use chemical-splash goggles;

- molten metals (melting lead)—use chemical-splash goggles;

- shaping of solid materials—chipping, hammering, cutting, grinding, sawing, etc. (rocks, minerals, glass tubing)—use spectacles or chemical-splash goggles;

- spraying and dusting (body fluids)—use chemical-splash goggles;

- projectiles and collisions (model rockets, broken glassware)—use spectacles or chemical-splash goggles;

- elastic materials under stress (springs, wires, rubber)—use spectacles or chemical-splash goggles;

- centrifugal devices (centrifuge)—use spectacles or chemical-splash goggles; and

- working with biological materials (dissecting, preserving, staining)—use chemical-splash goggles.

Get the Correct Goggles

Spectacles or safety glasses are normally used for protection from solid flying particles or fragments. The ANSI (American National Standards Institute) standard classifies safety glasses by the letters A, B, C, and D. Type A protects only against direct frontal flying fragments and therefore has no side shields. Types B, C, and D offer protection against flying fragments entering from the side through the use of side shields. All four types should be ANSI rated Z87.1 for impact protection. Science teachers should require use of ANSI Z87.1 safety glasses with protective side shields for appropriate activities.

Chemical-splash goggles are used for protection from hazardous liquids. These goggles fit snugly to the face with little or no space for liquids to infiltrate. The two types are G and H. Type G has no ventilation and type H provides ventilation. The ventilation is usually provided with protective hoods or caps over the vent openings. In both situations, goggles need to be rated Z87.1 for impact protection. Science teachers should require the use of ANSI Z87.1 chemical-splash goggles with indirect vents for appropriate activities.

ANSI Standards

When ANSI approved the new Occupational and Educational Personal Eye and Face Protective Devices standard—ANSI Z87.1-2003, it meant that eye protectors must be classified as either basic or high-impact. Basic-impact protectors must be capable of passing a one-inch drop ball test. These spectacles are to be marked with Z87.1 (basic-impact level). High-

impact protectors need to comply with high-mass and high-velocity impact criteria. If a lens meets the high-impact rating, the spectacle must be rated as Z87.1+ (high-impact level). Basic-impact level eye protectors are usually appropriate for middle school science activities.

Posting Signage

Most statutes require posting of appropriate signage to advise occupants on the need for eye protection. Laboratories and other sites where there is danger posed to the eyes are required to post notification, including statutes, warnings, list of hazards, and required protection. Teachers and administrators should contact local and/or state authorities to determine what signage is required in school laboratories and other locations.

Hygiene

Sanitation is required for safety glasses and goggles. This is especially important for eye protectors that are shared. Methods for sanitation include goggle sanitizers with ultraviolet lamps. Alternatives, though less effective, include soaking in hot water and antibacterial detergent, or using alcohol swabs. Headbands should also be inspected and replaced when they no longer provide the support needed to hold the spectacles or goggles in place. Lenses should not only be sanitized but also kept free of dirt and other particles that tend to block or blur vision.

6. Fire Safety Fundamentals

A student decided to have a little "fun" by starting a fire in the science wing of a school. He went into the boy's lavatory and cranked down the paper towels from a plastic dispenser. The bottom of the four feet of toweling was then ignited with a lighter. As the flames advanced up the toweling, the heat began to melt the plastic dispenser. The lavatory started to fill with thick, dark smoke, which was then carried to the science laboratories by the out-of-code ventilation system. The occupants of the building were immediately evacuated, but many still suffered irritated eyes and lungs. Firefighters were called to the scene, and a potential disaster was averted.

In another incident, students were using a Bunsen burner and a double boiler to extract chlorophyll from maple leaves. The leaves were placed in alcohol in a top beaker that was placed atop a larger beaker of boiling water. Unfortunately, the flame from the burner ignited the alcohol in the top beaker. A teacher who had been trained how to use a fire extinguisher quickly put out the flames.

Planning and prevention is the best defense against fires in school. This is particularly true in the science laboratory because of the presence of flammable gases, liquids, combustibles, and other potential sources of fire. Teachers can prevent fires from starting by maintaining prudent lab practices when dealing with combustible and flammable materials. It is also important for them to know how to handle fires if they start.

The Occupational Safety and Health Administration (OSHA) and the National Fire Protection Association (NFPA) regulate most aspects of fire prevention and response. OSHA General Industry standard 29 CFR 1910.38 addresses emergency planning, fire prevention plans, and evacuation plan requirements for employees. Additional standards addressing fire extinguishers are addressed in 29 CFR 1910.157. The NFPA Life Safety Code standards also address many aspects of fire prevention—such as occupancy loads, means of egress, and furnishings—in schools and science laboratories.

Extinguisher Class

The NFPA has classified fires into four basic types, depending on the source of the flame. Fire extinguishers are rated or classed based on these four types of fire sources. The class or classes of a fire extinguisher are displayed on the extinguisher in large, capital letters. Classes include the following:

- Type A: For fires involving combustibles such as paper, plastic, rubber, and wood. Water or dry chemicals extinguishers are appropriate for this type of fire. Carbon dioxide or extinguishers containing sodium or potassium bicarbonate should not be used.

- Type B: For flammable liquids and gases such as gasoline and alcohol. Carbon dioxide, foam, or dry chemical extinguishers can be used for this type of fire.

- Type C: For fires where electricity is involved such as computers and power supplies. Dry chemical and carbon dioxide extinguishers can be used for this type of fire. Foam and/or water extinguishers should not be used.

- Type D: For special combustible metals such as sodium, magnesium, and titanium.

- Type ABC: This type of extinguisher can handle A, B, and C types of fire sources. They are the most appropriate for the school science laboratory.

Remember that the wrong type of extinguisher can make a situation worst. For example, water from a Type A extinguisher can cause an explosion on a Type D metal fire. Fire extinguishers should be placed in a highly visible, easily accessible location. One extinguisher per lab is usually sufficient, but you may want two if you frequently conduct labs involving flammables.

How to Use PASS

In case of fire, the primary objective is to get all occupants out of the laboratory. Even if you consider the fire to be small and manageable, students should be trained to move toward the exit in case the fire escalates. If administrative or board of education policy includes employee use of fire extinguishers, employees must be trained annually by a firefighter or other professional safety trainer per OSHA regulations. Even with training, teachers should attempt to put out only fires that are small enough to be extinguished by a handheld extinguisher. When in doubt, vacate and contact the head office for assistance. Contact the office only while students are moving out of the room.

The most common approach to extinguisher use is the PASS system:

- **P**—Pull the pin on the extinguisher.

- **A**—Aim the hose at the bottom or base of the fire.

- **S**—Squeeze the trigger on the extinguisher.

- **S**—Sweep the hose back and forth.

There are several important things you should know before operating an extinguisher:

- Most extinguishers are only useful for about 8 to 10 seconds before they are empty.

- Attempt to use an extinguisher only

on small fires that can be quickly extinguished.

- Always have your back to an exit.

- If the fire is out of control or of unknown origin, leave it to the professionals by sounding the fire alarm and evacuating the building.

Preventing Fires

Good housekeeping is critical in preventing fires. Without it, the risk of fire and injuries and fatalities increases dramatically. Teachers and students can use the following strategies to keep the workplace clutter-free and prevent fires in the laboratory.

- Do not use any temporary wiring such as extension cords.

- Do not place electrical cords near water or heat or near combustibles or flammables.

- Do not use wires that are frayed or worn.

- Do not use plugs where the ground is broken off.

- Do not leave lit candles or operating burners and hot plates unattended.

- Do not work with a chemical until you have read the material safety data sheet (MSDS) and know the flash point (minimum temperature at which a liquid has enough vapors to ignite), flammable limits (concentration range of the material in the air in which it can ignite), reactivity, compatibility, and firefighting measures.

- Do not work with flammable liquids unless ignition sources (flames) are not present, there is good ventilation, and electrical devices in the area that might cause sparks are properly grounded.

- Do not forget to point out the location of the emergency gas shutoff valve to students.

- Do not work with compressed gases,

such as oxygen, unless the bottles of gas are anchored to a wall or support cart with belts or chains.

- Do not work in an area where there are no clear passages or fire doors available. Exit routes must be well marked, and you should have your students practice evacuating safely.

Extinguisher Maintenance

Remember to routinely check the gauge and expiration tags on your extinguishers. After using an extinguisher, ask the maintenance staff to replace or refill and charge the extinguisher that was used before any additional experimentation is done in the laboratory.

7. First-Aid Policies

Would you know what to do if one of your students had an accident with a chemical that resulted in contact with the skin? What would you do if a student spilled boiling water on his or her hands? These are the types of potential challenges science teachers face every time they walk into a laboratory with students. Unfortunately, not every science teacher is prepared to deal with situations that involve first aid. Are you prepared? Consider the following questions before you answer:

- Are science teachers required to provide first aid in their laboratories?

- Do science teachers need training to administer first aid to students who are injured?

- Should there be a first-aid kit in the science laboratory?

- If so, what should be in the first-aid kit?

Answers to these questions vary because of factors such as the instructor's level of formal training, available supplies, district policies, and medical support. Regardless of the answers, the first few minutes following a laboratory accident can be critical, so your school needs a comprehensive first-aid policy to guide employees in times of crisis.

When developing a first-aid policy, science teachers and supervisors should consider:

1. Occupational Safety and Health Administration Regulations: OSHA 29 CFR 1910.151 Subpart K Medical and First Aid standard requires the employer to ensure that their employees have ready access to medical personnel. Local and state departments of health require schools to provide medical support for students. If a medical facility such as a hospital or clinic is not readily available, someone on the job site must be adequately trained to administer first aid. For certification, teachers can enroll in formal first-aid courses through their local American Red Cross chapter or other certified training program.

2. OSHA 29 CFR 1910.151 Appendix A notes that first-aid supplies must be readily available. The supply list, taken from the American National Standards Institute (ANSI Z 308.1-1978), includes:

- adhesive bandage compresses,

- bandage compresses,

- triangular bandages,

- absorbent gauze compresses,

- gauze roller bandages,

- adhesive tape,

- metal splint,

- tourniquet, forceps, and scissors,

- eye-dressing packet,

- eyewash solution,

- ammonia inhalants,

- antiseptic swabs, and

- burn treatments.

3. OSHA 29 CFR 1910.151 Subpart K Medical and First Aid standard also requires the availability of eyewash stations and shower facilities for quick drenching or flushing of eyes and body when injurious corrosive materials (such as hydrochloric acid and vinegar) are used in the workplace. They must be accessible within 10 seconds from any part of the laboratory. They also must provide a minimum of 15 minutes continuous flow of tepid water.

4. OSHA also requires, in the same standard, a review of material safety data sheets (MSDSs) for all hazardous chemicals before using them in the laboratory. Also, keep copies of the MSDSs available on-site for easy access during an incident. The school nurse or other medical provider will need the MSDS information to help provide appropriate first aid to the victim.

5. OSHA notes that training of employees in first aid is not required if an EMT, nurse, physician, or first-aid certified individual is on-site or close by. The science teacher is the exception because of the corrosive materials used in the lab. Science teachers are required to receive initial responder training from the school nurse or other qualified professional to learn how to use safety equipment, such as the emergency eye-wash station, and how to care for accident victims until help arrives. If possible, science teachers should also receive formal first-aid training and certification from a group such as the Red Cross.

A medical responder must be able to reach an accident victim in a timely manner. In many, if not most cases, the time window is very small before permanent damage is done.

After any safety incident, follow board of education procedures to complete accident reports. Accident reports are used for insurance claims, OSHA reports, and any other legal activities related to the incident.

If a science teacher provides first aid without training, there is potential for legal action by the victim should there be permanent physical and/or psychological damage. In most cases, the school district's liability insurance would cover the actions of the teacher.

Typical safety incidents common to science laboratories requiring minimal first-aid training include

- bleeding (resulting from cuts and lacerations);

- burns (resulting from use of hot material such as burners, matches, and hot plates);

- chemical exposure (to substances such as acids and alkalines);

- lacerations (from broken glass or other sharp objects piercing or scraping skin);

- penetrating objects (such as projectiles and sharp hazards);

- shock (electrical); and

- swallowed poisons (such plants and chemicals).

In each case, while first aid is provided, the teacher should request immediate assistance from the school nurse or other medical care provider.

An additional source of data about workplace accidents is the OSHA 300 log. Employers are required to collect accident data and make that information available annually to employees. By reviewing the OSHA 300 log, additional items might be considered for the first-aid kit, such as latex or other suitable gloves for blood-borne incidents.

Reliable communications are essential to access medical support at a moment's notice. A telephone, cell phone, intercom, or another communication device is a must in the laboratory when it comes to accidents and securing medical support. Teachers are responsible for making sure the means of communication are in good working order. Keep the numbers for your local Poison Control Center and the school nurse's office next to your phone.

One more thought—Remember that the teacher can also be a victim in an accident. Students should be trained as to what action to take to secure help immediately. In most cases, students should be instructed to simply alert a nearby faculty or staff member and/or contact the school medical provider.

Internet Resources

American National Standard Institute—*www.ansi.org*

American Red Cross—*www.redcross.org*

Occupational Safety and Health Administration—*www.osha.gov*

8. First-Aid Response Essentials

Knowing the correct first-aid response to an emergency is critical in middle school science labs. The ideal protocol for a school district is to have all science teachers certified in first-aid training. Having said that, few if any school districts have policies or procedures that support such a protocol. From a practical standpoint, science teachers should be trained to respond to incidents involving burns, bleeding, chemical exposure, swallowed poisons, penetrating objects, lacerations, and shock. Basic training is required to properly handle these situations, and this training should be reviewed annually. Below is a list of possible lab incidents and the appropriate first-aid response. However, for each of these and for any other accident in the lab, request immediate assistance from the school's health care provider. In addition, review your school's first-aid protocol to see if it recommends an action that would supersede the advice given below.

A. **Heat and chemical burns:** It is possible that someone will get burned in the laboratory by such things as Bunsen burners, matches, and hotplates. Should that happen, immediately soak the burned area in cold water. Request immediate assistance from the school's health care provider.

B. **Electrical burns:** The severity of the burn depends on the type, amount, and length of contact. An electrical incident may also cause the heart to stop or to beat erratically. Respiratory arrest may also occur. Signs of electrical injury include unconsciousness, dazed and confused behavior, breathing difficulty, obvious burns on the surface of the skin, weakness, irregular or absent pulse, and burns both where the current

entered and where it exited. You can also suspect a possible electrical injury if a sudden loud noise such as a pop or bang is heard, or an unexpected flash of light is seen. If the teacher is trained or certified in CPR, initiate emergency care. Otherwise, request immediate assistance from the school's health care provider.

C. **Bleeding:** Bleeding can occur as a result of cuts from glass, metal, scalpels, and other sharp objects. In situations where arterial bleeding occurs, prompt action is required. Apply direct pressure over the wound with use of a barrier such as a rubber glove. If a glove is not handy, use a shoe with the hand inside of it. The barrier is needed as a standard precaution. Request immediate assistance from the school's health care provider.

D. **Chemical exposure:** With an increased emphasis on hands-on, process, and inquiry-based science, chemical exposure has a heightened probability of happening. Be certain to have the material safety data sheet (MSDS) available for each hazardous chemical used and review it prior to any laboratory work being done. Should there be an exposure, have the injured person immediately (within 10 seconds) use the eyewash or acid shower, as appropriate. Flush with copious amounts of tepid water for a minimum of 15 minutes. Request immediate assistance from the school's health care provider. Note that an eyewash and acid shower are required safety equipment for science laboratories!

E. **Swallowed poisons:** Accidental swallowing of poisonous chemicals in the laboratory can happen. It is critical to review MSDSs with students prior to use of these chemicals so all are familiar with their potential harm to the body. If the person becomes unconscious or is convulsing, do not induce vomiting. The same is true should the person complain of a "burning feeling" in their throat. Provide plenty of water or milk if available. Request immediate assistance from the school's health care provider. It is also wise to contact the Poison Control Center if you know what poison has been accidentally taken.

F. **Penetrating objects:** Using projectiles and walking in a laboratory with sharp objects can be hazardous and cause body punctures. Do not remove the object if a puncture occurs. Try to keep the individual calm and still. Request immediate assistance from the school's health care provider.

G. **Lacerations:** Broken glassware or other sharp objects can cause cuts. If bleeding occurs, try to have the injured person put on latex or NIOSH (National Institute for Occupational Safety and Health) approved plastic gloves and ap-

ply direct pressure to control bleeding. If that is not possible, make sure you keep a barrier (glove) between you and the injured person while trying to apply direct pressure. Request immediate assistance from the school's health care provider.

H. **Shock:** Symptoms of shock include faint pulse, clammy skin, nausea and/or vomiting, and increased breathing. The victim should be lying down with feet elevated. Cover with a blanket to keep warm. Request immediate assistance from the school's health care provider.

No matter what the incident, it is wise to immediately request assistance from the school's health care provider. In addition, check with your building principal in case the first-aid response protocol supersedes the recommended actions.

9. Hand Washing

The National Science Education Standards emphasize hands-on, process, and inquiry-based science. As a result, more students in today's middle school science classes are now exposed to a higher number and wider variety of laboratory activities. To ensure the health and safety of both students and teachers in science laboratories and fieldwork, personal hygiene protocols must be developed and followed. Hand-washing and hand-care practices are especially important and have long been recognized as a standard health and safety protocol for laboratory work.

Research findings strongly suggest a high correlation between the use of hands and the spreading of infection. In day-to-day science laboratory routines, touching objects can contaminate hands with microorganisms such as bacteria, viruses, and fungi. These organisms can gain access into our bodies and cause a myriad health-related problems. For example, general laboratory activities requiring the handling of equipment, supplies, and labware can cause bacterial contamination if skin is not intact (cut, dry, or cracked).

Students in biology laboratories working with soil, pond water, microorganisms, plants, and animals can come in contact with a variety of bacteria and other living things that have the potential to cause infections or other health-related problems. Chemistry laboratories can also expose students to hazardous chemicals and cause skin-related problems such as rashes and eczema. In addition, some students in today's schools have immune deficiency disorders, which are exacerbated by exposure to biological and chemical components in science laboratories.

The threat of exposure and contamination can be significantly reduced through the adoption of laboratory protocols. The following list covers hand-washing and hand-care elements that should be considered as part of prudent laboratory practice in the middle school science laboratory:

Hand-Washing/Hand-Care Protocol

- Wash hands with plain soap and warm water prior to working in the science laboratory. Soap should be available at each sink.

- Make sure the soap has a neutral pH with no added substances, such as perfumes. Additives and improper pH will cause irritation and dryness.

- Thoroughly lather hands, rubbing soap on all areas. Use caution not to scrub or scrape skin. Rinse hands with generous amounts of water.

- Dry hands by patting them with a soft and absorbent paper towel. Paper towel dispensers should be available at each sink.

- Avoid using electric hand dryers for laboratories. They are relatively expensive, they can pose an electrical hazard, and may harbor microorganisms.

- If bar soap is used, have it drain on a rack to facilitate drying. Make sure it does not sit in a pool of water. This scenario will foster the growth of bacteria in the soapy slime.

- Liquid soap dispensers can be used and placed next to each sink. Again, once emptied, the containers must be cleaned and dried before refilling with new liquid soap.

- To prevent contamination, make sure all hand cuts are covered adequately before beginning laboratory work with any biological or chemical agents to prevent contamination. There should be bandages over cuts, and hands should always be covered with gloves.

- Students and teachers with sensitive skin conditions such as eczema should always wear gloves.

At the End of the Lab

The last step in laboratory work should involve rewashing hands with soap and warm water. If students and teachers are exposed to bacteria, antibacterial soap may be necessary. However, continued use of these types of soaps tend to cause skin problems and destroy the natural hand flora (nonharmful and beneficial bacteria on the skin). Skin cells can also be destroyed, resulting in problems such as cracked skin, irritations, and rashes.

If gloves (latex—check for latex allergies—or vinyl) are used, hand washing is still required. Microorganisms and hazardous chemicals can penetrate through nicks, cuts, and pores in glove material. Soap and warm water are sufficient for most handwashing situations. Alcohol and other types of disinfectants are poor cleansing agents. Soap and other detergents break down "dirt" and should be used before introducing disinfectants.

For field work, use detergent-containing towelettes to clean hands. Towelettes are wet wipes, usually in a plastic container for easy use. A familiar example is the baby wipes found in most grocery stores and pharmacies. Detergent towelettes or wipes contain detergent—remember, the detergent is used first to loosen up the dirt. Almost any type of baby wipe can be used. Then, an alcohol or disinfectant can be used to destroy any remaining microbes. Some baby wipes contain both detergent and disinfectant. Students and teachers should be familiar with these practices and trained in proper hand-washing techniques.

Resources

Kwan, T., and J. Texley. 2002. *Inquiring safely: A guide for middle school teachers.* Arlington, VA: NSTA.

Centers for Disease Control and Prevention (CDC) at *www.cdc.gov*

Occupational Safety and Health Administration (OSHA) at *www.osha.gov*

10. Legal Prudence

A middle school science teacher was sued by the parents of two students who were poisoned by the mercury they stole out of the teacher's unlocked desk drawer. A group of parents sued another middle school teacher after they discovered the teacher instructed students to share lancets during a blood-typing activity. A third science teacher was sued by the parents of students who spilled acid on their face and arms and were burned because they were not wearing safety goggles, aprons, or gloves. You may think that these types of accidents could never happen in your lab, but accidents do happen even in the most controlled environments. So, the best thing you can do to protect yourself and your students is to implement and document proactive safety procedures.

Because science teachers are trained and licensed professionals, the courts expect that science teachers will have taken all possible actions to help prevent an accident from happening. A teacher's negligence or breach of a duty that results in a student's being exposed to unreasonable risk of harm is often the focus of litigation. Some actions that are recommended to reduce accidents in the lab and litigation in the courtroom follow.

Student Actions

The following are student actions that should be initiated by the teacher:

Laboratory safety training: Before beginning any laboratory work, science teachers should review safety in the laboratory, including general operating procedures (pouring chemicals, massing, and carrying), appropriate use of personal protective equipment (chemical-splash goggles, gloves, and aprons), and use of engineering controls (eyewash, shower, fire extinguisher, and master shutoff controls).

Safety contract: Once laboratory safety training is completed, present to and review with students a safety contract (see "Contract With Students," p. 38). Also share the contract with parents, and have them sign it. Keep original copies on file for at least one year following students' enrollment in a science course. In some rare cases, parents refuse to sign such documents. If they do, date, sign, and note the fact that the parent refused to sign the safety contract.

Safety test: Once the laboratory training has been completed, each student should be tested on safety content and skills learned. A high assessment bar, such as 90%, should be established. Retakes should be required until students have mastered the material. Again, date and keep either originals or copies on file up to one year after students leave the course.

Safety questions on tests and quizzes: Throughout the school year, include on tests or quizzes one or two safety questions that are either relevant to a laboratory activity completed or that are simply a review of basic laboratory training. Keep samples of these tests on file.

Safety drills: Periodically, conduct safety drills. For example, simulate a chemical-splash incident (using water as an acid) and have students demonstrate the proper response. These kinds of activities are fun for students and help to bring home the seriousness of a correct response during a safety incident.

Material safety data sheet (MSDS) reviews: Whenever hazardous chemicals are used in the laboratory (this could be something as simple as vinegar), the highlights of the MSDS should be reviewed with students, including precautions, health risks, and appropriate protective gear. The MSDS should also be made available at all times when the chemical is being used in the laboratory.

Teacher Actions

The following are actions the teacher should take:

Lesson plan logging: Lesson plans can become a legal document, so take advantage of them. Notations should be made relative to safety whenever any laboratory activity is written in the lesson plan book. This also includes safety training and review or relevant MSDSs.

Department meeting agendas: Most science departments meet once a month. Safety should be a standing agenda item. Discussion can focus on safety issues or skill training. Keep a record of the agendas and training items.

Professional training: Safety training programs are often offered throughout the country by professional science organizations, state departments of education, and private vendors, such as Flinn Scientific (*www.flinnsci.com*) and the Laboratory Safety Institute (*www.labsafety.org*). Try to attend formal training at least once every year or two. Secure a certificate and continuing education units. As with other safety initiatives, keep the records.

Professional safety resources: There are many safety resources available in print or on the internet. For example, the OSHA website (*www.osha.gov*) has many free safety items relative to laboratory work. Vendors such as Flinn have a middle school catalog that focuses on safety resources. The NSTA bookstore also has many safety resources available, such as *Inquiring Safely: A Guide for Middle School Teachers* (Kwan and Texley 2002). Make use of these resources and keep them in your professional library.

Laboratory signage: Safety signage is important in that it provides reminders and direction for appropriate behaviors in the laboratory. Make sure signage is available for fire extinguishers, fire blankets, master shutoffs, safety splash goggle use, and so on.

Protection

Science can and should be fun and exciting, but safety needs to be part of doing science. Teachers need to protect themselves and their students by being proactive and by fostering safe practices.

References

Kwan, T., and J. Texley. 2002. *Inquiring safely: A guide for middle school teachers.* Arlington, VA: NSTA Press.

Ryan, K. 2001. *Science classroom safety and the law: A handbook for teachers.* Batavia, IL: Flinn Scientific.

11. Space for Safety

The issue of science laboratory space and class size has been on a long safety trek. For example, the National Science Education Standards and subsequent science frameworks at the state level have emphasized the need to do science, not just read about it (NRC 1996). As a result, teachers have been engaging in more laboratory activities with their students. This action, coupled with increasing enrollments and outdated facilities, is once again putting science laboratory space on the radar screen. The bottom line is middle school science teachers must address *occupancy load*, more familiarly but less accurately known as class size, in efforts to establish and maintain a safe working and learning environment in the laboratory.

Occupancy loads are important in that they establish or engage the "load" factor for science laboratories in middle schools. Generally, science laboratories built for educational occupancies have loads established at 50 net square feet per occupant. (The net square footage of a lab is equal to the total square footage minus the amount of space occupied by cabinets, furniture, and other objects.) To maintain a safe working environment for both students and teachers, science laboratories at the middle school level must be analyzed to determine a design load for safe exiting capacity. Factors such as type of laboratory furniture, utilities, hazardous chemicals, sprinkler systems, and number of exits are considered in determining the occupancy load level.

When determining occupancy loads, science teachers first need to clearly differentiate between the terms *science classroom* and *science laboratory*. A science classroom is a place for talking about science. It is not a site for student experimentation under normal circumstances. A laboratory is a place for students to do science. A formal laboratory facility has hazards such as gas, electricity, hazardous chemicals, glassware, eyewash, shower, and more. Middle school science laboratories are classified as laboratories by safety standards from the National Fire Protection Association (NFPA), Building Officials and Code Administrators Association (BOCA), International Code Council (ICC), and Occupational Safety and Health Administration (OSHA).

Occupancy Loads are defined under Section 1008.1 of the National Building Code as "…the number of occupants for whom exit facilities shall be provided." The NFPA 101 Life Safety Code also defines occupancy load as "The total number of persons that might occupy a building or portion thereof at any one time." NSTA (National Science Teachers Association), state education departments, and others have established additional legal and quasi/professional occupancy standards.

Evacuation Plan

An effective plan of evacuation for all occupants of the science laboratory must be in place in case of an emergency. If a laboratory class size is over the design load, it does not meet the standard and is in violation. This would equate into an unsafe working environment for students and teachers. Science teachers must work with administrators and the local "authority having jurisdiction," such as the town fire marshal or state fire marshal, to correct the code violation.

Steps to Take

If your district is in the planning stages of new construction or renovations consider the following:

- Learn about NFPA, BOCA, and ICC occupancy codes applicable to science labs in your district. Local and state fire marshals and building inspectors are good sources for this information.

- Help write "educational specifications"

to better meet occupancy load design expectations and other safety components; such as fume hoods, acid showers, eyewash stations, and appropriate ventilation.

- Be an advocate by helping to educate administrators, board of education members and architects on safety needs in science laboratories, including occupancy loads.

Safety Is Your Job

As licensed professionals, middle school science teachers are held to a higher expectation in job performance by the legal system relative to safety in the laboratory and classroom. Science teachers must determine if it is unsafe to conduct certain experiments in their laboratories, based on safety codes and standards such as occupancy loads. You should plan alternative lab activities if this is the case in the short term.

In the long term, science teachers should work with administrators to improve laboratory safety. Remember that negligence and liability are issues that would be addressed should there be a laboratory accident. Be proactive by bringing your safety concerns to the attention of administrators in writing. Be supportive by working with them to make a safer working environment. If the administration is reluctant to take action, consider taking the matter up with your union. You might also consider contacting OSHA, parents groups, and in extreme cases, insurance companies for support.

References

National Resource Council (NRC). 1996. *National Science Education Standards*. Washington, DC: National Academy Press.

12. Classroom or Lab?

A newly hired middle school teacher was told by the principal that he would like her to develop a "laboratory-oriented" science course for the eighth-grade science program. She was excited about this curriculum charge and quickly began planning for the start of school. She returned to the school in August to visit her assigned science classroom. Much to her surprise, the room was a general classroom that had been used for study halls. There was no sink, no water, one electrical outlet, no eyewash or shower, no storage—just chairs, desks, and a blackboard. The teacher started questioning the curriculum charge of a "laboratory-oriented" science course. The principal said not to be concerned about the lack of equipment and materials. He told her to just do the best she could. In the days and months that followed, there was much make-do, and a very limited number of science activities.

Unfortunately, this is an all-too-common situation for science teachers. Science teachers worry about safety and professional liability in these cases and they should. The real question here is: What are the bare bones that must exist for a room to be considered safe for teaching laboratory science?

When Is a Lab a Lab?

What first must be considered is whether the room really is a laboratory. Can it be used for laboratory activities? Is it safe? Is a middle school science laboratory considered to be a real science laboratory and therefore subject to safety standards? According to the Occupational Health and Safety Administration (OSHA) (#29 CFR 1910.1450, Occupational exposure to hazardous chemicals in laboratories), "*Laboratory* means a facility where the laboratory use of hazardous chemicals occurs. It is a workplace where relatively small quantities of hazardous chemicals are used on a nonproduction basis." Given this point of reference as a generic definition, minimally, the school as an employer should provide a well-equipped laboratory and a chemical safety plan for science instruction that involves the use of hazardous chemicals. Middle school general science laboratories fall under this model and are therefore considered real science laboratories.

A chemical hygiene plan should require all sites designated as laboratories to be specifically noted in the plan. In this way, there will be no question in the minds of employees as to what are their safety protocols and standard operating procedures. These operations are in effect when hazardous chemicals are present or in use. Other restrictions may also be applied by the employer. Therefore, school officials need to carefully consider situations in which science laboratories have students and nonscience-certified teachers assigned to science laboratories for general study classes or other nonscience activities. In addition, special training should be provided for custodians assigned to clean science laboratories.

Basic Safety Standards

Now that the term *laboratory* is defined, what safety equipment and materials should be there? First of all, it will depend on what kinds of science activities are being done by teachers and students. OSHA states that the safety equipment and materials must fit the activity or work being done. For example, if students are going to use hazardous chemicals—even something as simple as vinegar—eye protection in the form of chemical splash goggles, aprons, gloves, eyewash stations, shower, and signage is required. If electricity is used, circuits should be protected by a ground fault circuit interrupter (GFCI). This goes for things like aquariums, ripple tanks, and so on. If gas is used as a heat source via burners, a master gas shutoff system is required. Laboratories also require one-way ventilation; that is, the air cannot be recycled at all and new air must be provided at a minimum of eight room changes per hour occupied and four room changes per hour unoccupied.

The Environmental Protection Agency in Region 7 has listed an outline of the basic safety equipment/procedures for school science labs as follows:

1. *Training.* Teachers should be trained to identify potential hazards, evaluate potential hazards, and prevent or respond to hazards.

2. *Material safety data sheets (MSDS).* Maintain a copy of the MSDS for every item in the chemical inventory. This information helps teachers determine important facts about chemicals, such as storage, handling, disposal, and appropriate protective equipment.

3. *Safety glasses/goggles.* Safety glasses or chemical-splash goggles should be used during all activities in which chemicals (chemical-splash goggles) or particles (safety glasses) may accidentally enter the eye. Review and consider the types of hazards present when selecting appropriate eye protection. Eye safety equipment must provide protection for the risks involved in an activity.

4. *Gloves.* Many chemicals can damage the skin via contact or if allowed to be absorbed through the skin. Protective gloves serve as a barrier to prevent skin problems. Also, remember that different hazards require the use of different gloves.

5. *Aprons.* Aprons are designed to provide protection in the event of a splash or spill.

6. *Eyewash units.* Eyewash stations should be provided in all areas where chemical or physical hazards may cause eye irri-

tation or injury. Do not use temporary bottled eyewash units. Only permanently plumbed units are acceptable.

7. *Deluge showers and fire blankets.* Deluge showers and fire blankets should be maintained in all areas where chemical or fire hazards exist that may result in partial body exposure. Appropriate signage is critical also.

8. *Fire extinguishers.* ABC-type fire extinguishers should be maintained in accordance to state and local fire and building codes. The correct size and type of extinguisher is determined in accordance with the materials commonly used or maintained in that space.

9. *Ventilation.* Additional mechanical ventilation such as chemical fume hoods should be provided in all areas where chemical fumes, vapors, or odors are commonly generated. Sufficient ventilation should be provided to prevent the buildup of hazardous air contaminants and to minimize nuisance odors.

10. *Spill kits.* Spill kits and carts need to be available to address and respond to chemical spills of substances such as acids and bases.

11. *Chemical storage cabinets.* The bulk storage of hazardous materials may necessitate the use of reinforced chemical storage cabinets or storerooms. Flammables, corrosives, oxidizers, and similar items need dedicated and secured storage.

Meeting Safety Needs

Science lessons involving discussions, lectures, group work and some types of activities that don't use material or equipment are OK for a general classroom. For example, the room mentioned in the introductory paragraph—a study-hall room—is appropriate for these instructional strategies but inappropriate for doing most science activities. In order to do science, personal protective equipment and engineering controls are required when potentially dangerous materials are used or procedures are done. Something as simple as using metersticks requires eye protection!

Some teachers have to deal with the "science on a cart" concept. Again, it all depends on the level of the dangers associated with the activities. There are very simple types of activities with common materials that normally are safe to use with minimal concern. On the other hand, there can be activities which require full-blown laboratory safety equipment. Again, this is where safety training is important so the teacher knows how to be aware of the dangers, assess the level of the dangers, and take appropriate action to prevent accidents. Remember the triple As of safety—Awareness, Assessment, and Action!

Students must be able to *do* science in order to learn science. With appropriate safety precautions, doing science can be fun and safe. Science is different from most other disciplines in that it requires attention to the risks involved and a proactive attitude toward safety.

Resource

EPA Region 7 Lab Science Safety Equipment Requirements for Middle Schools—*www. epa.gov/region7/education_resources/teachers/ ehsstudy/ehs14.htm*

13. Contract With Students

Student safety contracts are an important tool for teachers to use in helping to prepare for and maintain a safe working environment. They also serve as an additional way to show that the teacher was working in good faith when dealing with safety issues, should litigation be on the agenda.

It is a good idea to have parents or guardians sign off on the contract, along with the student. Parents need to be aware of the school's effort to establish and secure a safe working environment in the science laboratory. This action makes the parent aware of the importance placed on safety and potential ramifications should the student break the contract. Parents should be made aware of behavioral expectations and enforcement that might include removal from the lab, detention, and academic consequences. In rare instances, parents or guardians may refuse to sign the contract. Should this be the case, teachers should simply make a note on the student's form stating the fact that the parents or guardians refused to sign after reading the contract.

The internet has many examples of safety contracts. The following is one such example that is used at Smith Middle School in Glastonbury, Connecticut, for physical science courses. Laboratory contracts should be customized for your school, division of science, sophistication of the laboratory, and other factors. This sample only serves as a guide or point of reference:

Laboratory Science Safety Contract

1. The science laboratory can provide you with the exciting opportunity to do science. However, remember at all times that the laboratory is a place for serious work. Fooling around or disruptive behavior can result in removal from the laboratory.

2. Always prepare for an experiment by reading the directions in the manual before you come to the laboratory. Follow the directions carefully and intelligently, noting all precautions. Do not add to, omit, or change any of the directions unless your teacher instructs you to do so.

3. Do only the experiments assigned or approved by your instructor. Unauthorized experiments are prohibited.

4. When working with corrosive materials, chemical-splash goggles, gloves, and lab aprons must be worn throughout the lab period until all your classmates have completed the lab and the chemicals are safely stored. When the teacher's protective equipment is on, your protective equipment is on. When the teacher takes off his or her protective equipment, you can take off your protective equipment.

5. Do not touch chemicals with your hands.

6. Never taste a chemical or solution. No food or drink is allowed in the laboratory classroom.

7. When observing the odor of a substance, do not hold your face directly over the container. To observe safely, fan a little of the vapor toward you by sweeping your hand over the top of the container.

8. Allow ample time for hot glass to cool. Remember that hot glass looks like cool glass.

9. Know the location of the blanket station, eyewash, and the fire exit procedure. In the rectangle on the other side of this page, diagram the lab areas noting the locations of all safety equipment, exits, fire alarms, etc. Note the location of the Chemical Safety Plan and material safety data sheet (MSDS)

envelope for the experiments.

10. Know the location of your school's Chemical Safety Policy and the MSDS. MSDS information must be shared with students by the instructor or read by students, specifically those sections detailing handling precautions, disposal techniques, and other pertinent information for each chemical.

11. Report any accident, even a minor injury, to your instructor.

12. Discard all waste from lab activities into a chemical waste jar or other location specified by the teacher in accordance with MSDS instructions.

13. Read the label on any chemical bottle you are planning to use in a lab to verify that it contains the correct chemical. Do not use any chemicals stored in unlabeled bottles.

14. Never return unused chemicals to the stock bottle. Do not put any object into a reagent bottle except the dropper with which it may be equipped.

15. Keep your apparatus and work area organized. Avoid spillage, but if you do spill something, notify the teacher and clean up the spill immediately using the appropriate technique.

16. During clean-up time, attend to your

Science Department Policy and State Statutes

Any person who is working, teaching, observing, supervising, assisting or engaging in any work, activity or study in a public or private elementary or secondary school laboratory or workshop where the process used tends to damage the eyes or where protective devices can reduce the risk of injury to the eyes concomitant with such activity shall wear an eye protective device of industrial quality in the manner in which such device was intended to be worn. When in doubt, wear chemical-splash goggles.

To maintain a safe working environment for all occupants, teachers are required by the district safety compliance officer to remove from the classroom any student out of compliance. This is for your own protection and that of students.

❏ I have read the attached safety rules and have been present when they were discussed in class or I discussed them directly with my science teacher.

❏ Yes, I wear contact lenses.

I have allergies/sensitivities to: _____

Print name _____

Student signature _____

Class _____ Date _____

Instructor _____

I have read and discussed the laboratory safety rules with my child.

Parent signature_____Date _____

assigned area duties. All duties must be completed before leaving the laboratory. Wash hands thoroughly with soap at the conclusion of each lab.

17. Respect your equipment and fellow laboratory workers.

18. Handle all spring-loaded and projectile devices with extreme caution to prevent accidental release or discharge. (See number 22.)

19. You are not allowed to work in a laboratory unless an instructor is present. All student experiments are to be done under the direct supervision of an instructor. Students completing science project assignments at home must complete a permission form before any work is begun, and a parent or guardian must sign the form.

20. Open-toed shoes and sandals, loose-fitting clothing, and jewelry are not permitted during laboratory activities. Long hair must be tied back securely during laboratory activities.

21. Books and notebooks are to be stored under your desk or table for clear aisles and exiting. No backpacks are allowed.

22. Science department regulation and state statutes require that all students, teachers, and visitors in the laboratory must wear chemical splash goggles during work periods, including clean-up time.

▽ CHEMICAL SAFETY

14. Chemicals— What's In?

Mention the word *chemistry* in a middle level classroom and the first thing students want to know is, "Will we be blowing anything up?" Chemistry should be fun and exciting, but teacher and students need much preparation and skill for working with chemicals. Unfortunately, accidents do happen and things can blow up, but you can help prevent these incidents by knowing and following proper safety procedures. Knowing which chemicals are appropriate for the middle level classroom is a good place to start.

Some chemicals, though still found in middle school inventories, are considered too hazardous to store and use. Unfortunately, some school science curricula require experiences in labs or demonstrations that have made our "what is out" list. Should this be the case, extreme caution, preparation, planning, personal protection equipment (PPE), appropriate facilities, and proper disposal are all required.

The Occupational Safety and Health Administration's (OSHA) Laboratory Standards requires the employer in most states to develop a chemical hygiene plan (CHP). The CHP should address chemical use or nonuse policy with input from science employees. This is a good starting point for professional dialogue on the appropriate selection of chemicals for use in the middle school.

What to Use

The following chemicals can be considered for use in hands-on middle school science programs. However, you should review the character of each chemical or compound by consulting the appropriate material safety data sheet (MSDS). Appropriate precautions, such as PPE and ventilation, are an absolute must for safe use of any and all chemicals. Please note that this brief list represents the most common types. There are other chemicals that can be considered safe. MSDSs need to be reviewed before use. Note also that all acids and bases listed are in a dilute, not concentrated form.

- activated charcoal (carbon)
- Alka-Seltzer tablets
- alum (several compounds containing aluminum and sulfate)
- aluminum foil (aluminum metal)
- ammonia water (aluminum hydroxide)
- baking powder (sodium aluminum sulfate)
- baking soda (sodium bicarbonate)
- beet or cane sugar (sucrose)
- borax (sodium borate)
- boric acid
- calcium chloride salt (calcium chloride)
- chalk (calcium chloride)
- club soda (carbonic acid)
- copper wire (copper metal)
- corn starch
- cottonseed oil
- cream of tartar (potassium bitartrate)
- denatured alcohol (ethanol)
- epsom salts (magnesium sulfate)
- flowers of sulfur (sulfur)
- fruit sugar (fructose)
- glycerin (glycerol)
- grape or corn sugar (glucose)
- graphite (carbon)
- hydrogen peroxide solution (hydrogen peroxide)
- iron filings (iron metal)
- olive oil

- plaster of paris (calcium sulfate)
- rubbing alcohol (propanol 2)
- salt (sodium chloride)
- table salt (sodium chloride)
- table sugar (sucrose)
- vinegar (acetic acid)
- vitamin c (ascorbic acid)

What NOT to Use

The following list represents common chemicals that may be found in middle school science labs or storerooms and should be removed due to their hazardous nature. Remember that any chemical can be considered hazardous if not used appropriately. Again, consult the MSDS for additional information.

- ammonium dichromate—$(NH_4)_2Cr_2O_7$ (toxic byproducts)
- benzene (carcinogen)
- calcium carbide—CaC_2 (explosion hazard)
- carbon tetrachloride—CCl_4 (carcinogen)
- chloroform—$CHCl_3$ (carcinogen)
- concentrated inorganic/mineral acids such as hydrochloric acid—HCl, nitric acid—HNO_3, sulfuric acid—H_2SO_4 (all are a corrosive, serious burn and eye hazard)
- copper sulfate (toxic)
- diethyl ether (forms explosive peroxides)
- dry ice—carbon dioxide (frostbite and blisters)
- elemental mercury—Hg (highly toxic)
- elemental potassium—K (forms explosive oxides)

- elemental sodium—Na (dangerous reactions with water)
- formaldehyde—HCHO (carcinogen)
- hydrogen sulfide—H_2S (toxic vapors)
- iodine—I_2 (respiratory irritant)
- lead compounds such as lead chloride—$PbCl_2$, lead nitrate—$Pb(NO_3)_2$ (one or more are potential carcinogens, toxic)
- magnesium strips—Mg (burn hazard)
- mercury salts such as mercuric sulfate—$HgSO_4$ (toxic)
- methanol or methyl alcohol—CH_3OH (toxic)
- mineral talc—$Mg_3Si_4O_{10}$ (can cause asbestosis)
- picric acid—2,4,6-trinitrophenol (explosive crystals)
- potassium chlorate—$KClO_3$ (can cause violent reactions)
- silver cyanide—AgCN (toxic)
- sodium hydroxide—NaOH (caustic)
- vinyl chloride—$CH_2=CHCl$ (carcinogen)
- white phosphorous—P (fire hazard)

The study of chemistry concepts and hands-on chemistry activities belong in the middle school science curriculum. Teachers need to make sure they understand and respect chemicals by being informed. Often, simple substitutes can work just as well as a chemical that presents a safety concern. Be on your guard by using the first line of defense—the material safety data sheet.

Resource

Kwan, T., and J. Texley. 2002. *Inquiring safely: A guide for middle school teachers.* Arlington, Va.: NSTA Press.

15. Dealing With Spills

OSHA's (Occupational Safety and Health Administration) Occupational Exposure to Hazardous Chemicals in Laboratories or the Laboratory Standard requires a chemical hygiene plan to address all aspects of working with hazardous chemicals. This includes dealing with chemical spills. Chemical spill kits or "spill crash carts" must be available in case there is a spill incident in the laboratory.

The first line of defense against a chemical spill is to try to prevent one from happening. Effective means of prevention are to provide training and to use minimal amounts of hazardous chemicals. The microchemical approach has merit in terms of safety alone. Appropriate storage, use of containment devices, inspection of containers, and other things can again help keep the chances of a spill accident very low.

As advocated by the National Science Education Standards, however, there should be virtually no use of hazardous chemicals in the middle level classroom.

Plan of Attack

In working with chemicals, material safety data sheets (MSDSs) are critical. They can provide the information to help determine if the user has been exposed to toxic or caustic substances and to give direction about appropriate decontamination or first responder action. For example, if a student has acid splashed on his or her skin, decontamination should take place by using the emergency shower in the laboratory. If the splash is localized on the hands, tepid water from a sink will suffice.

If the spill is on the lab facilities and not on a person, you must first decide if it can be handled at the building level or if the fire department or other emergency personnel must be called in. Extremely hazardous situations, such as a gas leak, may require immediate evacuation from the building prior to the arrival of the emergency crews.

For the spills that can be safely addressed by the instructor, take the following steps:

- Review the MSDS for spill-control information before working with any chemical so you know what to do immediately if an accident occurs. Keep the sheets close by for quick reference.

- Have someone notify the administration immediately. A spill can be addressed by the instructor as long as it is controllable—for instance, if ventilation can handle it, it can be contained easily, volatile fumes are not being released, or you have materials to pick it up.

- Make sure you have the appropriate personal protective equipment available for cleaning up spills. See "Keep on the Crash Cart," p. 45.

- Avoid exposure to fumes by opening windows or turning on exhaust fans. After the cleanup has been completed, ventilation should remain on to remove any lingering vapors.

- Wash hands with soap or detergent.

- Label recycled or hazardous material to identify contents, date, location, and cleanup person. It should then be properly removed and disposed of according to MSDS recommendations.

Dry spills involving chemicals such as calcium chloride and sodium bicarbonate can be swept up and placed in a recycling or hazardous waste container. Label the container appropriately.

For liquid spills, such as acids and bases, containment is required. An acid or base neutralizer from the spill kit, such as sodium carbonate or calcium hydroxide, should be poured around the perimeter of the spill, working inward. A scoop can then be used to transfer the slurry to a hazardous waste container for disposal.

For spills of volatile organic solvents such as alcohol, which can be very dangerous, evacuation is usually required. Cover the spill with an absorbent from the spill kit, such as sand or kitty litter. Extinguish all flames and shut off the gas and sources of electrical sparks such as circuit breaker panels.

For nonhazardous liquids, such as water, use absorbents such as sand or kitty litter. Add kitty litter, allow the liquid to be absorbed, and then sweep it up and dispose of it with your general refuse.

Mercury

Should there be a mercury spill, take the following steps:

- Provide maximum ventilation by opening windows and doors and turning on exhaust fans.

- Put plastic over shoes to prevent contaminating other areas.

- Push the "islands" of mercury together using the collection tool in your clean-up kit. Pick up the mercury with a spill tool or medicine dropper into a seamless polyethylene or polypropylene bottle. The remaining mercury can be picked up with a mercury sponge (do not use a broom or vacuum cleaner).

- Consult with state department of environmental protection to determine how to treat a mercury spill of your size. Usually, if the amount is larger than a quarter, the department may need to be called on site for the cleanup.

Spill on a Person

For small spills on the skin, wash the affected area for several minutes with tepid water. Consult the MSDS to determine if there are any residual effects from the chemical, such as irritation or redness. Secure medical attention from a school nurse. If the spill is extensive, make use of the chemical safety shower. If none is available, rinse the victim's affected areas as thoroughly as possible in a sink using tepid water.

For spills on clothing, the clothes should be removed as quickly as possible. Provide a blanket for the sake of modesty, but don't delay the removal of the contaminated clothing. The following procedure is recommended:

- Direct other occupants to leave the room.

- Remove footwear and jewelry to ease washing.

- Use a chemical safety shower for no less than 15 minutes. Make sure the shower is provided with tepid water (acceptable range is 60–100°F).

- During the shower, keep eyes tightly shut to prevent chemical exposure.

- Avoid exposure to vapors from any spilled material by increasing ventilation such as opening windows or turning on exhaust fans.

- Resume shower for as long as needed (or until medical responder arrives) if, after the 15 minutes of showering, the person is still in pain.

- Get medical attention, such as the school nurse, as soon as possible.

- Have the MSDS available for the medical responder.

- Make sure there is access to an eyewash station for chemical splashes in the eyes. The station must supply tepid water for a minimum of 15 minutes. Remove contacts if present. Try to hold the eyelids away from the eyeball while gently moving the eyes up, down, and around. Secure medical support from the school nurse.

Keep on the Crash Cart

Chemical spill kits or spill crash carts are critical for a quick response to a chemical incident. The following supplies are recommended for spills:

- absorbents such as sand or kitty litter,
- apron,
- broom and dust pan,
- chemical-splash goggles,
- mercury sponge,
- mop and bucket,
- neutralizing agent such as sodium carbonate (washing soda),
- paper towel,
- plastic garbage bags,
- rubber gloves, and
- sponges.

Spill carts should be placed for easy and quick access. Ideally, there should be one in each laboratory.

Resource

Kwan, T., and J. Texley. 2003. *Inquiring safely: A guide for middle school teachers.* Arlington, VA: NSTA Press.

16. Storage and Disposal

One of the most essential but difficult responsibilities of new science teachers is the proper inventorying and storage of laboratory chemicals. "Difficult" because few new science teachers have had the formal training in college to deal with appropriate storage of laboratory chemicals. "Essential" because the Occupational Safety and Health Administration's (OSHA) Laboratory Standard (29 CFR 1910.1450) and Hazard Communication Standard (29 CFR 1910.1200) require appropriate procedures to be established for safe use of hazardous chemicals, including storage in the work environment by employees.

Additionally, new science teachers may inherit more than just "the wind" when they walk into their assigned laboratory. Veteran science teachers have been known to leave behind a nightmare of chemical baggage when they retire. Scenarios abound of dented cans, broken bottles, leaking containers, unlabeled and undated chemicals, alphabetically organized chemicals, overloaded shelves, and chemicals left in the back of cabinets and under the fume hood. These artifacts become the legal responsibility of the new occupant.

Serious attention must be given to the safe storage of laboratory chemicals in all middle school science laboratories. Before storing chemicals, inventory your supplies and make decisions about what they need for instruction and what they can remove and dispose of properly. The following is a list of prudent practices for chemical storage that I have compiled over the years. It should prove useful to both new and veteran middle level science teachers in getting a handle on the storage situation.

Prudent Practices

- Chemical storerooms are considered secured areas with access restricted to only licensed science teachers, trained custodians, and administrators (no student access).

- Chemicals must be inventoried and dated on the original container upon receipt.

- Chemicals should be stored by compatibility (families), not alphabetically—for example, store them by metals and hydrides; acids, alcohols, and glycols; hydroxides and oxides.

- If at all possible, do not store chemicals above eye level and never store acids higher than the bottom shelf.

- Make sure shelving is secured to walls to prevent toppling over—never cover circuit breakers or other essential power shutoffs with shelving.

- Shelving should have lips to prevent containers from rolling or falling off.

- Chemicals need to be examined periodically for expiration, deterioration, and container integrity.

- Chemical storerooms are just that—for storage, not for preparation.

- All chemicals are to be properly labeled at all times, including chemical name, hazard classification/hazard warning, manufacturer name and address, and emergency phone number.

- Chemical storage refrigerators must have appropriate signs and must not be used for storing food or drink.

- Chemicals stored in laboratories must be in relatively small amounts and secured.

- Corrosive chemicals must be stored separately from flammable, combustible, and reactive chemicals.

- Corrosive chemicals must be stored in approved corrosive cabinets and labeled "CAUTION, CORROSIVES."

- Flammable or combustible chemicals

must be stored only in cabinets for flammable storage approved by the National Fire Protection Association (NFPA) with "FLAMMABLE" labels.

- Flammable or combustible chemicals requiring refrigeration must be stored only in an Underwriter Laboratory–approved, explosion-proof refrigerator.

- Have one or more fire extinguishers Class ABC in the chemical storage area.

- Storage area ventilation systems must be isolated from general laboratory and other building ventilation systems.

- Storage area ventilation should effect a minimum of four room changes per hour. Seek help from the school district's maintenance foreman or an outside contractor to make sure the lab meets this standard.

- Fume hoods should not be used for chemical storage.

- Chemical-spill stations containing dry sand and other spill control materials must be established.

- Smoke and heat detectors should be installed in the chemical storage area.

- An eyewash station and fire blanket should be located near the storage area.

- Material safety data sheets (MSDSs) must be secured and stored in an area of easy access for all chemicals in the inventory.

- Toxins and carcinogens should not be in the middle school science inventory.

Internet Resources

Flinn Scientific (good source for Material Safety Data Sheets)—*www.Flinnsci.com*

Occupational Safety and Health Administration—*www.OSHA.gov*

Oklahoma State University Environmental Health and Safety—*www.pp.okstate.edu/ehs/links/labchem.htm*

17. Purchasing Protocol

Within recent years an urban school district had planned to dispose of some hazardous chemicals. It contracted with a chemical recycling company that was considered to be reputable. The school district, along with several other companies, was charged and fined by the Environmental Protection Agency for improperly releasing hazardous chemicals into the environment. The recycling company had simply dumped the chemicals with their containers in a local river.

In another case, a suburban school district had hired a chemical recycling company to package and remove a small cache of hazardous chemicals. The company came to the school to package the chemicals and discovered an error in the quote for the job. The company tried to charge the school district several thousand dollars extra for two chemicals already listed on the quoted price manifest. The district refused, claiming unfair business practice. Before the unscrupulous company pulled out of the site, it took all the valuable chemicals and left in their place hazardous chemicals they had collected from other sites. The school district ended up having to spend several thousand additional dollars for another chemical recycling company to appropriately dispose of the "newfound" chemicals.

The bottom line of these two scenarios is the cost of buying hazardous chemicals does not stop with the initial purchase. Buyers need to be prepared to pay additional amounts for appropriate disposal of those same chemicals. With this in mind, schools need to consider adopting a protocol for the purchase, storage, use, and disposal of chemicals.

Purchase and Use of Hazardous chemicals

Most hazardous chemicals have no place in the middle level classroom. If you have an activity that calls for a hazardous chemical, and you can't find a safer alternative, consider these purchasing guidelines. The first rule of thumb is to buy only what you'll need to get you through the year. Buying in bulk may save you money, but storing the excess materials creates a safety hazard. The second rule is to use the least-hazardous chemical available that will still allow you to meet your teaching objectives. Both of these rules can be achieved by adopting "microscale chemistry" and "green chemistry" approaches to instruction (see p. 87).

The material safety data sheet, or MSDS, should be consulted for disposal procedures before you purchase chemicals. Consider carefully that chemicals requiring inexpensive disposal methods rather than those chemicals that have costly disposal methods. Generic MSDSs for this purpose can be found on the internet (check the Resources at the end of this article).

Before using a chemical, make sure the MSDS is read and all instructions concerning ventilation, storage, use, and other matters are obeyed. Also before using a chemical, share the MSDS information with students. Make sure they know how to use MSDS information as part of responsible laboratory practice.

Effective chemical management includes knowing what you have, how much you have, how old it is, what the "drop dead" or shelf-life date is, and where it is stored. A "living" chemical inventory is one that is kept up-to-date. Inventory systems can range from paper-and-pencil lists for small collections to spreadsheets and commercial computer chemical inventories for larger collections.

MSDSs need to be easily accessible, especially during chemical use in the laboratory. Keep MSDSs posted in the laboratory for chemicals being used during a class. Should there be a chemical emergency, access to these sheets is critical for medical-support responders like the school nurse or physician.

Storage of Chemicals

Properly store chemicals in appropriate locations—chemical storeroom, containers, cabinets, and so on, based on chemical properties and hazard information provided by the MSDS. Also, make sure when purchasing chemicals that MSDSs are provided with the chemicals as required by law.

General storage guidelines for hazardous chemicals include the following:

- Store chemicals based on compatibility using families or groups; e.g., avoid contact or storing of acetic acid near nitric acid. Flinn Scientific has a highly successful storage system that can easily be adopted.

- Make sure all stored chemicals have labels with information about the chemical name, manufacturer's name and address, and the health and physical hazards of the chemical.

- Make sure all storage areas are secured with locks and signage; such as "Hazardous Materials."

- Corrosives like acids and bases should be stored in a corrosive cabinet.

- Flammables like alcohol should be stored in a flammable liquid cabinet.

- Store hazardous chemicals in areas designated and secured for that purpose. Never store them on the floor, on a counter, in a refrigerator dedicated to consumable food goods, or in the fume hood.

Disposal of Chemicals: Way to Go!

The less hazardous a chemical is, the easier the method of disposal. A limited number of chemicals considered nonhazardous can be environmentally and legally safe to dispose of down the drain or in the refuse bin. Improper disposal in sanitary drains, however, can create serious health and safety problems. For example, crosscontamination can occur in laboratory sinks used for food and chemical preparation and lead to accidental ingestion. Chlorine-based products can generate noxious gas in drains. Indoor air quality can be affected if materials are trapped in the drain and release emissions over time.

Nonhazardous waste usually can be disposed of in small quantities (limit to a few hundred grams or milliliters) in this way. Flush these quantities with large amounts of water for high dilution. Remember that incompatible chemicals should not be comingled.

Chemicals such as acids and bases should be neutralized before you dispose of them. For example, acids can be diluted with water to a concentration of about 10% acid. To avoid splashing, remember to Always Add Acid to the water (AAA), and never the reverse. Gloves, an apron, chemical-splash goggles, and a fume hood or proper ventilation are also mandatory. Once diluted, the acid can then be neutralized by adding sodium carbonate until the pH reaches 7. Inorganic salts with nontoxic anion and cation components can also be disposed of down the drain if they are soluble. You'll need to check a disposal guide, such as the one published by Flinn (see Resources), to determine what specific actions are required. Always check with the water-treatment plant superintendent to make sure this is acceptable and to secure prior permission for disposal. Drain disposal is prohibited where septic systems and dry wells are in use. Check with your science supervisor or janitorial staff to see if this is the case.

Using the inventory system, the "drop dead" or shelf-life list tells you when chemicals must be recycled or disposed of. Many chemicals will decompose over time, becoming contaminated, discolored, and inappropriate for use. Chemical products from reactions also need to be considered on the manifest list for removal. First, determine which chemicals on the list are hazardous and which are nonhazardous waste, based on MSDS information and other resources. Make sure all waste is appropriately labeled or identified with contents, dates, and so on. Unlabeled bottles of waste will be costly to remove.

Chemicals determined to be hazardous need to be professionally handled by hazardous material waste contractors. Many towns provide free household hazardous waste disposal programs and are willing to include school chemicals. For commercial disposal, check with the state Better Business Bureau relative to any complaints lodged against waste contractors before hiring them.

KISS

Keep it simple silly, or KISS, is the message of the day for purchase, storage, use, and disposal of chemicals. Remember that the purchaser owns the chemical, even after its disposal. That means if the chemicals are inappropriately disposed of, fines will be levied against the original owner or purchaser for appropriate cleanup.

Resources

Flinn Scientific—*www.flinnsci.com*

Occupational Safety & Health Administration (OSHA)—*www.OSHA.gov*

MSDS Search: National Repository site—*www. msdssearch.com/msdssearch.htm*

Kwan, T., and J. Texley. 2002. *Inquiring safely: A guide for middle school teachers*. Arlington, VA: NSTA Press.

18. Mercury Spills

Recently, a senior center was closed after a mercury spill at a high school. The reason? Two students who had been exposed to mercury from broken thermometers while doing an experiment in their science class visited the center to perform in a concert. Fearing contamination, the center was closed and tested. Another incident in a large city school involved students entering an unsecured chemistry laboratory after school and taking elemental mercury. The students contaminated many areas of the school, requiring it to be shut down for several weeks. A third instance involved the renovation of several high school laboratories. Science textbooks from these laboratories were stored in a trailer over the summer. Unfortunately, someone also stored an open bottle of mercury in the same trailer. The heat vaporized the mercury and the vapors permeated the textbooks. All of them had to be replaced and the resulting cleanup and damage costs were estimated to be over $250,000! These are only a few examples of relatively recent incidents involving the mishandling of mercury.

Problems With Mercury?

Mercury tends to vaporize when exposed to air. The warmer the air, the more quickly it vaporizes. Although swallowing mercury can be a problem, the greater risk results from inhalation and skin absorption. Symptoms and health-related problems can result within hours of exposure.

Short-term or acute exposure symptoms include

- difficulty in breathing,
- coughing,
- nausea and vomiting,
- diarrhea,
- fever, and
- metallic taste in the mouth.

Long-term or chronic exposure symptoms include

- loss of appetite,
- sleeping difficulty,
- irritability,
- shakiness,
- memory loss,
- headache,
- emotional instability, and
- psychological changes.

Spilled mercury settles in cracks and absorbent material such as carpet, wood, draperies, and cloth. Over time, the vapors are emitted and inhaled by occupants. Remember, the problem with mercury is that it keeps on recycling itself. It vaporizes, is absorbed by materials in the environment, and again vaporizes. It is a problem that persists until there is intervention!

Locations of Mercury

In science laboratories, mercury is found in thermometers, pressure gauges, mercury compounds, and elemental mercury. However, sources of mercury are present beyond the science laboratory. Locations in schools can include

- thermostats,
- silent wall switches,
- fluorescent lamps, neon lamps, and high-intensity discharge lamps,
- old microwave ovens,
- batteries,
- latex paint produced prior to 1992,
- pesticides produced before 1994,

- blood pressure gauges or sphygmomanometers, and

- thermometers.

Why Use Mercury?

Science teachers have used mercury for decades, if not longer, for demonstrations and laboratory experiments. Compared to most other elements, mercury is unique. For example, mercury

- is the only metal that is liquid at room temperature,

- easily evaporates into the air and can be absorbed by other materials,

- is an excellent conductor of electricity and used in many electrical devices,

- is used in thermometers because of its ability to change volume uniformly with changes in temperature,

- readily kills bacteria and mold,

- has exceptionally strong cohesive forces, and

- forms compounds, such as mercuric oxide, that can easily produce oxygen gas.

Safe Alternatives

Yes! The major source of mercury can be found in thermometers. Alcohol or electronic thermometers should replace all mercury thermometers. Mercury thermometer exchange programs can be found at the local and state level, commercial hazardous waste vendors, and science laboratory equipment and supply houses. There are also sufficiently accurate alternative devices to mercury barometers, vacuum gauges, manometers, and sphygmomanometers. Nonmercury alternatives include electronic or digital gauges and aneroid barometers. Less hazardous chemicals can be used for demonstrations and experiments in science. If mercury compounds are prescribed or required, the microscale approach is advised.

Handling Spills

In many school districts, the size of the spill will dictate the response level. To prepare for a spill, find out the mercury cleanup protocol from your school's administration or board of education. General mercury spill guidelines are available from a number of sources including most state departments of environmental protection and the federal Environmental Protection Agency.

For spills resulting from a broken thermometer or gauge break with less than two tablespoons of mercury, take the following actions:

- Evacuate occupants from the laboratory or classroom and secure the area to keep others out.

- Prevent the spread by keeping any clothing, shoes, and other materials that have come in direct contact with mercury at the spill site.

- Ventilate the room with outside air by opening windows and using fans to avoid breathing in vapors.

- Turn off or segregate the heating, ventilating, and air conditioning systems to prevent the spread of vapors.

- Keep the site cool by lowering thermostats in efforts to reduce the rate of vaporization.

- Close interior doors to reduce the chance of recirculation of vapors.

- Remove all jewelry that may have come in contact with the mercury (mercury will bond with metals such as gold).

- Use rubber gloves to prevent contact with the skin.

- Never clean up a mercury spill with a broom or vacuum cleaner, which fosters vaporization.

- Never pour mercury down the drain because it will remain in the plumbing and vaporize into the air.

- Use an eyedropper, stiff paper, or duct tape to scoop the mercury into a container.
- Remove affected carpeting and store as contaminated material for disposal.
- Label any collected mercury as "hazardous mercury spill cleanup materials," including the date and location.
- Have the mercury disposed of as hazardous waste.

For spills greater than two tablespoons, immediately contact your school administrator. He or she in turn should contact a professional spill vendor, local fire department, state department of environmental protection, or other professional spill responder as noted in your district's protocol.

The internet is the best resource for up-to-date mercury information. The U.S. Environmental Protection Agency is an excellent source for information. Its website is at *www.epa.gov*.

19. Why You Need an MSDS

OSHA's (Occupational Safety and Health Administration) Hazard Communication Standard (HazCom) requires chemical manufactures to provide material safety data sheets (MSDSs) for hazardous chemicals. Because hazcom is considered a performance standard, it does not require a specific format for the MSDS. But the MSDS must be in English and contain a minimum of required information about the hazardous chemical being used. An MSDS must be available for any chemical that presents a hazard to employees in the workplace.

Professional training of hazardous chemical users is necessary and required by OSHA. Communicating the hazards and handling of chemicals is the bedrock of the HazCom program. Part of the training must focus on how to read an MSDS sheet so it is understandable. OSHA is emphatic about going beyond simply giving an employee an MSDS to read. Simply handing the MSDS to an employee does not satisfy the spirit or intent of the standard for training.

An MSDS contains much information for health and safety of employees and students in the science laboratory. OSHA Form 174 lists the sections that are mandatory for MSDS information. Remember, this is only the minimal information. The American National Standards Institute (ANSI) has published a voluntary standard with 16 sections. Most MSDS formats reflect this standard. The information here will help science teachers, supervisors, and administrators better understand what information is required on an MSDS. An "R" indicates sections required by OSHA. The presentation follows the suggested ANSI format.

MSDS Information

Section 1—Product and company identification. This section provides information about the chemical manufacturer, including emergency contacts. In addition, product information, such as code and registration numbers, may be provided.

Section 2—Composition/information on ingredients. Active and inert chemical hazard ingredients and the Chemical Abstract Service (CAS) number are provided. Equally important are the OSHA permissible exposure levels (PELs) and American Conference of Governmental Industrial Hygienists (ACGIH) threshold limit values (TLVs) provided.

Section 3—Hazards identification. Potential health effects—acute (immediate exposure effects) and chronic (long-term exposure effects).

Section 4—First-aid measures. What first-aid measures should be taken should the chemical get into the eyes, onto the skin, be breathed into the lungs, or swallowed.

Section 5—Firefighting measures. Firefighting measures such as procedures, explosive limits, flash points, and more.

Section 6—Accidental release measures. Evacuation procedures, spill containment, and cleanup and disposal.

Section 7—Handling and storage. Storage temperatures, minimizing potential storage hazards, and reducing risk by proper handling.

Section 8—Exposure controls/Personal protection. Measures to reduce likelihood of swallowing, eye invasion, and skin contact; engineering requirements, such as ventilation; and personal protection, such as eye protection and gloves.

Section 9—Physical and chemical properties. Properties such as pH, color, odors, and vapor density.

Section 10—Stability and reactivity. How stable or unstable a chemical is and compatibility and incompatibility.

Section 11—Toxicological information, Consequences of short-term and long-term exposures to chemicals.

Section 12—Ecological information. The environmental fate of the chemical.

Section 13—Disposal considerations. Disposal directions and limitations.

Section 14—Transportation information. Shipping information relative to hazardous materials.

Section 15—Regulatory information. Regulatory requirements for OSHA, Toxic Substances Control Act, Resource Conservation and Recovery Act, and more.

Section 16—Other information. Additional information, such as National Fire Protection Association (NFPA) ratings, would be listed here.

Sample MSDS Information

Vinegar, or diluted acetic acid, is often used for its acidic properties in middle school science laboratory experiments. So, what information out of the MSDS would be helpful to plan for a safe activity?

Section 1—The name of the company providing the acid and the toll-free emergency number.

Section 2—Acetic acid, with synonym vinegar. Also identifies CAS number.

Section 3—Strong odor, colorless, corrosive, fumes can be suffocating.

Section 4—First-aid procedures for the eye—immediately flush for 15 minutes—and for inhalation—remove to fresh air at once.

Section 5—Use ABC-type extinguisher.

Section 6—Contain a spill with sand and absorbent material, neutralize with sodium bicarbonate or calcium hydroxide.

Section 7—Store with acids. Keep away from nitric acid.

Section 8—Wear chemical-splash goggles, chemical-resistant gloves and apron. Use appropriate ventilation.

Section 9—Soluble in water, vapor density 3.52 that of air, freezes at slightly below room temperature.

Section 10—Avoid contact with strong oxidizers like nitric acid. Indefinite shelf life if stored correctly.

Section 11—Acute effects—harmful—corrosive.

Section 12—Not available.

Section 13—Check with local regulatory agencies, U. S. Environment Protection Agency, and state department of environmental protection.

Section 14—Shipping information provided.

Section 15—Regulatory codes provided.

Section 16—None provided.

This information provides direction for the science teacher and can help him or her better prepare for a safer laboratory activity.

20. Plan Your Purchases

Your school district legally owns hazardous laboratory chemicals from cradle (point of purchase) to grave (final resting place). This means that should a science teacher incorrectly dispose of hazardous laboratory chemicals, there is the real opportunity for litigation from state and local health departments, the Environmental Protection Agency, and other chemical monitoring authorities.

For example, should a science teacher have students pour an inappropriate chemical down the drain after an experiment, that chemical action could cause a major bacterial kill in the local water treatment plant or septic system. Inappropriate chemical disposal on school property in a sports field could cause risk exposure for the whole school population. The chemical contaminant can seep into the water table for schools that use well water. A dumping of laboratory chemicals in a town landfill or transfer station can again cause contamination and problems for the science teacher and school district. All of these examples are real-life incidents relative to chemical disposal from schools.

Planning Ahead

Planning chemical use and disposal is critical to a safe laboratory environment. It is irresponsible to simply go out and purchase laboratory chemicals without considering why they are needed and how they will be disposed of when they are no longer needed. An OSHA-based (Occupational Safety and Health Administration) chemical hygiene plan (CHP) should be adopted by the science department as the first step. The CHP addresses procedures and operations for the purchase, use, storage, and recycling of hazardous chemicals. In other words, before chemicals are secured, review the need and life cycle of the chemi-

cal. Think "cradle to grave" when making purchases. Questions in planning might include:

- Is there a cheaper and less hazardous alternative that could be used in a microscale chemistry format or student activity kit?

- Is an up-to-date chemical inventory system in place?

- How much of the chemical will be needed?

- Where can the chemical be stored?

- How long can the chemical be stored?

- What precautions are needed in dealing with the chemical—such as engineering controls, personal protective equipment, and administrative policy?

- How will the chemical be disposed of after use?

- Is there a "chemicals to be recycled" program in place.

- Is there appropriate storage available for temporary holding of chemical items to be recycled?

- Is there appropriate ventilation for temporary storage of chemical items to be recycled?

- What type of water treatment process does the school use for items that go down the drain (dry well, septic, water treatment plant)?

- What local, state, and federal regulatory laws apply to chemical recycling?

Biological Waste/Recycling Materials

Waste from life science activities such as preserved materials, sharps, dead organisms, and so on may contain harmful organisms or toxic chemicals. First, consult the material safety data sheet (MSDS) for appropriate disposal methods. Again, planning before purchase will save much time and money in dealing with any items that need to be recycled. The temptation to throw biological waste/recycling materials into the trash is ever present. This can be a very dangerous practice. If sharps like dissection needles, razor blades, and so on are to be disposed of, use appropriate sharp disposal containers that are commercially available. Some schools use petri plates and grow bacteria or mold. These types of activities are not advocated, but, if you do use them, disposal necessitates sterilization in a pressure cooker, microwave, or autoclave. Also, appropriate labeling and packaging are required. Preserved materials or dead organisms present a special challenge, given that they are sites for bacterial or mold growth. Local colleges and industry can be tapped to incinerate remains. Licensed waste disposal companies are also available. The local municipal or town waste or refuse department can also be contacted for information about policies and recommendations on removing waste of this type.

Chemical Waste and Recycling

Issues unfold quickly when chemical reactants produce products that need special attention when recycled or stored. Stick with experiments and demonstrations that you are familiar with and that require the least hazardous chemicals. Stay away from heavy metals (such as mercury and lead)

and organic compounds (such as alcohols, aldehydes, and ketones) that require very specialized methods of recycling. When dealing with any chemicals, plan on a centralized collection system for items to be recycled. Keep it simple by using non-hazardous chemicals in your middle school laboratory.

There are a variety of methods that are used in recycling chemicals, such as dilution, drain disposal, neutralization, heating, evaporation, and removal to a landfill. The key is to learn which is appropriate for each particular chemical or compound.

Planning minimizes chemicals to be recycled. Also, make sure that chemicals that cannot be easily disposed of are removed by a licensed waste-disposal company. As licensed professionals, science teachers have the responsibility and duty to help save and reclaim the natural environment. This can be done by using appropriate recycling techniques and being chemically responsible.

An excellent resource for minimizing chemical use and disposal is the Flinn Scientific Company Science Catalog Reference Manual. Flinn has developed a user-friendly resource for science teachers dealing with a wide variety of chemical disposal and recycling methods.

Internet Resources

Flinn Scientific—*www.flinnsci.com*

Writing a chemical hygiene plan—*www.osha. gov/SLTC/laboratories/index.html*

▽ PHYSICAL SAFETY

21. Glassware Care

It is found in just about every school science laboratory. It comes in different shapes and sizes. It is transparent and can shatter easily. Yet it is versatile—it can be heated, cooled, and molded. It can be used to measure volume, contain reactions, measure temperature, evaporate salts, and transfer liquids or gases. It is glassware!

Interestingly enough, a study done several years ago indicated that more than half of the science laboratory accidents reviewed involved glassware. However, the risk of injury can be greatly reduced if the appropriate safety guidelines are followed. The following list reviews prudent practices in dealing with glassware in the middle school science laboratory. Students need to be part of these practices through training and application.

Glassware Safety

Inspection—Before using glassware, do a visual inspection. Most injuries with glass result from skin abrasions or lacerations due to sharp edges. Check for defects such as cracks or chips, rough or sharp edges, and bubbles in the glass. Should any defect be present, dispose of the glassware item.

Cleanup—If glass is broken, never pick it up with bare hands. Use only thick gloves, along with a broom and dustpan. Dispose of glass in the appropriate discard container. Small portable vacuum cleaners also are handy in getting up any little pieces of shattered glass that might be missed using a broom and dustpan.

Disposal—Any broken or defective glass should be placed in a special glass disposal container located within the laboratory. A thick-walled plastic garbage can works well. The container should be labeled "Glass Discard Only!"

Broken and defective glassware should not be placed in the regular classroom trash basket where it can cause injury to the unsuspecting user. For ease of removal, the container should have a plastic bag liner (construction grade, minimum of 2.0 mil thick). The bag should be removed only by trained custodial or maintenance personnel.

Intended use—Each type of glassware is designed for specific applications. For example, a flask would not be used to heat a liquid because its narrow neck could lead to a buildup of pressure and hot liquid could erupt from the flask. A better choice would be a beaker or watch glass.

Appropriate glass—Glass is often subjected to a large range of temperature changes—hot and cold. Borosilicate glass such as Kimax or Pyrex is designed to resist breaking under temperature changes. Regular glass, such as the type used to make drinking glasses, will shatter under this stress. Make sure the glassware being used for heating or cooling is labeled as Kimax or Pyrex.

Hot glass—Unfortunately, hot glass and cool glass look the same. If at all possible, do not leave hot glass unattended. If it is, leave a "Hot Glass!" note alongside it. Hot glass radiates heat, which can be felt by placing a hand near the glass but not touching it. If it is necessary to handle the hot glass, use beaker tongs, hot pads, or special heat gloves.

Storage compatibility—Glass bottles are great for storing most chemicals because of the transparent character of the material. However, carbonates and hydroxides are incompatible with glass and will etch it over time. Plastic containers can be used in these cases. Material data safety sheets, or MSDSs, can be helpful in determining reactivity characteristics.

Cleaning—At the middle school science

level, dishwashing powder or detergent is usually sufficient to clean glassware. After you have washed the glassware with the detergent solution, follow up with a clean-water rinse and drain for drying. For stubborn stains, use a glassware brush. A word of caution: Be careful that the metal part of the brush does not scratch or otherwise compromise the glass being cleaned.

Manipulating glass—People who are working with glassware must wear safety glasses. If hazardous chemicals (including hot water) are being used, chemical-splash goggles are necessary. If glass tubing must be broken, follows these steps:

- Scratch the glass using a file.
- Use a towel to wrap the glass.
- Put thumbs together opposite the scratch.
- Push and bend the glass with a quick jerking motion away from your thumbs.
- Heat the broken ends of the glass to fire-polish them smooth.

Sealing glassware—In some cases, an experiment may require glassware to be sealed. Rubber stoppers are used to seal aqueous solutions in glass vessels and corks to seal organic solvents. If a thermometer or glass tubing needs to be inserted through the cork or stopper, the teacher, not the student, should deal with this procedure. For inserting glass tubing or a thermometer, follow these steps:

- Use gloves to protect the hands.
- Make sure the hole in the cork or stopper is the correct size.
- Use a small amount of glycerin to lubricate the hole.
- Guide the glass through the stopper using a twisting motion. Be careful not to force the glass tubing or thermometer beyond its breaking point.

Glassware is an important part of doing science. Appropriately training students about its use will help provide a safe and successful laboratory experience for them. Better your students are sharp in dealing with glassware than working with glassware and getting an injury.

22. Safer Heat Sources

As heat sources go, the old standby for elementary and middle school science laboratories has been the centuries-old alcohol lamp. Unfortunately, this inexpensive heat producer has been a continuous source of accidents—many of which are serious. One of the most common accidents occurs when refilling the empty burner reservoir using a stock bottle of alcohol, and the still-glowing embers of the wick ignite the ever-present alcohol vapors. In most cases, students and teachers receive serious burns on the face, hands, and arms from the vapors bursting into flames. In some cases, the flames cause disfiguring injuries that require plastic surgery. Even more serious is the potential for the highly flammable vapors to explode. Another common accident occurs when a lit alcohol lamp is inadvertently dropped on the floor and the glass container breaks. This allows the flame to extend over a very large area with potential for a major fire.

Given these real concerns about alcohol lamps and the relatively high frequency of accidents, many states have issued safety warnings and even prohibitions against the use of alcohol lamps in the science laboratory. So are there any viable alternatives for heat sources? Yes! Depending on the amount and consistency of heat needed for middle school science experiments, there are at least three alternatives for consideration: electric hot plates, candles, and laboratory gas burners.

Good Source of Heat

Hot plates are emerging as the most popular source of heat for science experiments. The temperature can be controlled within limits. There is no direct flame or threat of explosion. Certain procedures, however, should be followed for safe operation.

Always demonstrate and enforce the following behaviors when working with hot plates:

- Use hot plates that have thermostatic controls.

- Visually examine the hot plates' electrical components, such as wire and plug, to make sure they are intact and the insulation is not compromised.

- Plug the hot plate into a ground-fault circuit interrupter (GFCI) to prevent shock.

- Heat test tubes by placing them in a heat-resistant—Kimax or Pyrex, for example—glass beaker of water on the hot plate. Make sure there is water in the beaker—never boil dry.

- Keep the open end of test tubes pointed away from everyone to prevent splashing.

- Use heat-resistant gloves or tongs to handle hot objects.

- Turn off the hot plate and then unplug it when finished.

- Remind students that hot plates remain hot long after they have been shut off and need to be handled with caution.

- Require students to make sure their hot plates are shut off before they leave the laboratory.

Bunsen Burners

Although there seems to be increased attraction to hot plates as heat sources, some middle school instructors still use and prefer the gas burner. The burner has a 150-year history going back to around 1855 when German chemist Robert Wilhelm Eberhard von Bunsen brought the gas-air burner into use. Many science laboratories use the Bunsen burner today as a heat source. The big plus with a Bunsen burner is that the amount of heat can be regulated. The downside is that the source can be very dangerous if not used correctly. When using these burners, follow these safety protocols.

For the teacher:

- Know where the gas emergency shutoff valve is in the classroom and instruct students how to use it.

- Make sure the gas jets are shut at the end of each use and that the gas is shut off entirely at the main valve at the end of the day.

- Check each burner before students light it to make sure that the air and gas are adjusted correctly, so that there will not be a flare-up when the burner is first lit.

- Show students the correct lighting procedure with whatever lighting tool they will be using—match or a flint striker.

- Make sure all chairs and items are off the floor when burners are in use and that the papers students bring to the lab station are kept to a minimum.

- Remind students where the ABC-rated fire extinguisher and fire blanket are located.

- Turn off the main gas supply at the end of each activity/class.

For students:

- Review all safety procedures for using gas before beginning any lab.

- Tie back long hair before working with the burner.

- Do not wear loose-sleeved clothing or sweatshirts with drawstrings. Natural fabrics such as cotton are flammable. Many synthetic materials are either flammable or will melt on the skin. Some, such as polar fleece, have been chemically treated, making them even more flammable.

- Put on chemical-splash goggles before

starting the laboratory activity.

- Know the location of the fire blanket and fire extinguisher(s).

- Remove flammable substances such as paper from the lab station before igniting the gas. The proper sequence for lighting the gas is to turn the gas on and then ignite the stream using a flint striker.

- Use only safety tubing that has been checked for leaks to connect the burner to the gas valve.

- Adjust the amount of gas and air to get the desired flame.

- Never place objects other than the glassware in the flame. Rubber and plastics can emit very noxious fumes when put into the flame.

- Secure a test tube to be heated in the flame with a test tube holder. Or, put the test tube on a ring stand with a test tube clamp.

- Always point the test tube away from others to prevent splashing with hot fluids.

- Evenly heat the test tube over the flame by moving it back and forth.

- If heating a beaker, use a ring stand to support the beaker with water in it.

- Extinguish burners when away from the work area. Verify that no flame is present and that no odor of gas can be detected. Report any gas odor immediately.

- Have a heat-resistant pad on the counter nearby to use as a surface for hot objects removed from the heat.

- Before picking up any glassware, place your hand near it to determine if it is cool. Hot glassware looks just like cool glassware.

- Allow all equipment to cool off before putting it away.

Candles

Candles can be an alternative heat source. As with other heat sources, certain precautions are necessary for safe use. Hot wax can cause a painful burn. Always follow these procedures with candles:

- As with burners, make sure to have appropriate fire protection and personal protection equipment on hand.

- Select candles that are wide and short. Their lower center of gravity helps prevent the candle from falling over.

- Use a drip pan such as an aluminum pie plate to catch the flowing wax and contain the candle should it fall over.

- Use beaker or test tube tongs and gloves when handling hot materials.

- Extinguish the flame when you are finished with the candle or when you are away from the work area.

- Allow all equipment to cool off before putting it away.

- Clean up any residual wax spilled in the work area that may have eluded the drip pan.

Resource

Kwan, T., and J. Texley. 2002. *Inquiring Safely: A Guide For Middle School Teachers*. Arlington, Va.: NSTA Press.

23. Using Heat

Laboratory work in the middle school often requires a heat source. For example, heating water to dissolve salts requires a heat source. But not every lab activity requires a flaming Bunsen burner. The following is a review of heating options for the middle school classroom and the guidelines for using the equipment safely.

Heating Basics

The only containers you heat should be made of borosilicate glass, such as Pyrex. All other types of glass, including the soft glass used to make graduated cylinders, can crack and shatter when heated. If labware shatters, it exposes students to glass shrapnel and hot liquids.

One of the greatest dangers in heating liquids or gases is the buildup of pressure and the ensuing explosion. Use only open containers, such as beakers and flasks with large openings, that allow vapors to vent freely. Never use reagent bottles or volumetric flasks, which have very narrow neck openings that could cause a problem. Bottom line: Never use a closed or nearly closed container—it can result in an explosion!

- If you select a burner as the heating source, use wire gauze on a ring, secured with a clamp. Do not use wire gauze with a white flaky pad—it is asbestos and very dangerous.

- When using a heating source, make sure there are no flammable or combustible materials nearby.

- Have a means of moving the heated vessel by using hot pads, thermal gloves, or tongs.

- Always wait for hot glassware to cool before touching it. Remember that hot glass looks just like cool glass!

- With all lab work, make sure proper protective equipment is used—chemical-splash goggles, aprons, gloves, tongs, and heat pads.

The Most Common Heat Sources

Several different heat sources can be used, depending on what is being heated.

Hot plates: This is an increasingly popular means of heating materials in the middle school science laboratory. A hot plate is used when controlled temperatures are needed. It can be used to heat up a liquid, solid, or gas. Hot plates should be plugged only into a circuit protected by a ground-fault interrupter (GFI). This protects the user from being electrocuted should there be a liquid spill resulting from the heating interacting with the electrical source.

- Review heating basics section.

- Use only hot plates with grounded or three-prong plugs with an Underwriters Laboratories, or (UL), listing.

- Keep the hot plate clean and dry.

- Inspect the wiring for damage.

- Use caution in handling the hot plate—it could still be hot from a previous user.

- Keep all electrical cords away from water and the heating surface of the hot plate.

- Keep wood, rubber, plastic, and similar materials away from surface of the hot plate.

- Turn off and unplug the hot plate when finished working.

Gas burners: This is the classic heating source that is used more often in high school or college laboratories. There is less control relative to specific temperatures and other inherent dangers associated with use of a flammable gas. This group includes Bunsen burners, Tyrell burners, portable propane, and butane burners. Heating organic liquids such as alcohol with a gas burner is very dangerous, and a fire can develop. The burner should be limited to primarily heating only nonflammable solvents, such as water, or aqueous solutions, such as saltwater.

- Review heating basics section.

- Before lighting the gas burner, tie back long hair, make sure you are wearing short or tight-fitting sleeves, and use chemical-splash safety goggles.

- Use only the appropriate burner type for the gas source—for example, never use natural gas when bottled gas is called for.

- Know the location of the master gas shutoff control. Make sure it is operational before using the gas.

- Use only burner tubing connectors that meet the American Gas Association or (AGA) standards. Do not use latex tubing.

- Inspect the burner and hose for any defects.

- Use only ceramic-centered wire gauze on the tripod—never an asbestos-centered pad.

- Use a safety lighter or match to light the burner. Carefully bring the flame up the side toward the top of the barrel while slowly turning on the gas.

- Shut down the burner immediately if the gas lights at the base of the burner.

- Adjust the flame to the appropriate height and color; e.g., medium-blue flame.

- Remember the gas burner is metal and will get hot. Do not handle the gas burner until the metal cools.

- Do not lean forward or reach over the flame.

- Do not leave the flame unattended.

Alcohol burners: Several states have prohibited the use of traditional alcohol lamps with metal caps and wicks. This is with good reason! The National Science Teachers Association (NSTA) does not recommend using alcohol burners for any lab activities. Numerous accidents have resulted from exploding vapors, and students and teachers have been burned. If alcohol lamps must be used, the wickless alcohol burner is a much safer alternative. Alcohol lamps should not be used in the primary grades.

- Review heating basics section.

- Do not bend over the burner. Keep all body parts, hair, clothing, and accessories away from the burner.

- Make sure the base of the burner is on a level surface.

- Shut down the flame when the burner is not in use.

- Do not light an alcohol burner directly from another lit one.

- Do not add alcohol to a lit or hot burner.

- Do not allow the tank to get overheated.

Candles: Many instructors do not like to use candles for heat sources. Like other heating sources, candles can be dangerous; e.g., clothing catching on fire, burning skin from hot wax, and so on. Most students will use candles at some point in their lives and should know how to do so safely.

- Review heating basics section.

- Trim the wick to about ¼ inch each time before burning.

- Place candle in a stable support on a

heat-resistant surface.

- Candles should not be used where there are strong air currents, drafts, or vents.

- Extinguish a candle if it smokes or the flame becomes too high. Check the size of the wick and for the presence of air currents.

- Burn candles only in a well-ventilated laboratory.

- Discontinue use of the candle when only 2 inches of wax remains (½ inch if the candle is in a container).

- Never touch liquid wax.

- Lit candles should always be within direct view. Never leave a burning candle unattended.

Hot water baths: This is a combination of hot water and either a hot plate or Bunsen burner. A beaker with water is heated with another beaker sitting inside it. The goal of this setup is to get the material inside the inner beaker heated to the same temperature as the water inside the outer beaker.

- Review heating basics section.

- Make sure the water bath is on a stable base (flat tabletop) to help prevent spills.

- Use a nonmercury thermometer so the bath temperature can be visually checked. Keep the temperature below 158°F or 70°C to prevent large-scale evaporation and boiling.

- Do not move the apparatus until the liquid inside has cooled down.

- Be sure to unplug the apparatus (if a hot plate is used as the heat source) before filling or emptying.

Resource

Journal of Chemical Education Chemistry Comes Alive! Video clips about heating safety at *http://144.92.39.64/JCESoft/CCA/ CCA0/C6/C6101000101.html*

▽ BIOLOGICAL SAFETY

24. Bloodborne Pathogens

Malaria, Lyme disease, Epstein-Barr syndrome, meningitis, syphilis, hepatitis B and HIV/AIDS—what do all of these diseases have in common? They belong to a group of more than 100 microorganisms categorized as *bloodborne pathogens*. Until the advent of AIDS, the general public tended to be unconcerned about these pathogens. With the HIV epidemic and public awareness of Hepatitis B, coupled with confidentiality legislation, bloodborne pathogens came on the public's radar. Bloodborne pathogens also got the attention of middle and high school science teachers, because of hands-on activities such as cheek cell staining and observation and blood typing, along with general exposure to dried blood or fresh blood.

What Are Bloodborne Pathogens?

A bloodborne pathogen is a microorganism such as a bacteria or virus that is carried, replicated, and/or transmitted in blood or blood products and is capable of causing disease in people. The Occupational Safety and Health Administration (OSHA) rang the alarm about the seriousness of these microbes by issuing in 1992 the Required Occupational Exposure to Bloodborne Pathogens standard (29 CFR 1910.1030), which was updated and revised in 2001. The standard mandates that employers institute a comprehensive program to prevent or reduce worker exposure to blood and other infectious materials. This standard applies to all employees, including science teachers, who may come in contact with blood and other potentially infectious materials as part of their job. In the case of the science teacher, the standard requires that the employer (the board of education) devel-

op a written bloodborne pathogens plan, train personnel annually, develop prudent work practices, provide personal protective equipment, foster safe workplace behaviors, and use engineering controls.

How Does Exposure Occur?

Exposure or transfer of bloodborne pathogens can occur in four different ways—direct, indirect, airborne, and vectorborne:

- Direct—Touching body fluids from an infected person. This includes contact with lesions, open wounds, or sores on the skin. Skin lining of the mouth, nose, or throat, and eye contact and invasion are additional avenues.

- Indirect—Touching objects that have touched the blood or another body fluid of an infected person. This includes touching broken glass with blood on it, clothes with blood stains, or other items.

- Airborne—Coming in contact with spores or other pathogen transfer mechanisms that are traveling through the air.

- Vectorborne—Receiving a bite from an insect that is serving as an incubator for the pathogen.

  The vehicles of transfer include

- needle sticks;

- cuts from contaminated sharps, such as scalpels and broken glass;

- sharing of needles during drug use;

- contact of mucous membranes—for example the eye, nose, mouth—or broken—cut or abraded—skin with contaminated blood;

- sexual contact; and

- mothers to babies during pregnancy or during breast feeding.

Universal (Standard) Precautions

All human blood and potentially infectious body fluids should be treated as infected. Because of confidentiality legislation, a science teacher will not know if his or her student has a bloodborne pathogen.

All body fluids containing visible blood and certain other body fluids such as saliva, cerebrospinal fluid, semen, vaginal fluids, and amniotic fluid, should be considered contaminated. Other more common body fluids are not normally considered contaminated, but may be. These include nasal secretions, sputum, urine, and vomitus.

OSHA requires a written exposure control plan that is accessible to employees. The plan must include an annual review and employee training, amongst other things. It also requires the employer to provide engineering controls (sharps disposal containers, retracting lancets with safety features), work practice controls (no food in work areas, washing hands with soap after removing gloves), personal protective equipment (gloves, chemical-splash goggles), and good housekeeping practices.

Remember that human skin normally provides an excellent barrier to bloodborne pathogens. But open sores, cuts, abrasions, acne, or any kind of damaged or broken skin such as sunburn or blisters can provide access for bloodborne pathogens.

Dealing With Them

There are direct ramifications for the science teacher when dealing with bloodborne pathogens. Examples include, but are not limited, to the following:

- **Blood typing:** Blood typing activities used to be done in both middle and high school science laboratories. With the advent of OSHA's Bloodborne Pathogen Standard, schools have dropped this activity, given the potential risk of exposure to students and employees. In addition, synthetic blood–typing kits provide a viable alternative. It is not prudent practice for a middle school science class to be doing human blood typing.

- **Cheek cells:** Middle school life science classes also used to do cheek cell staining and observation as an introduction to body systems. Again, the risk is too high at this point. It is prudent practice to use alternative preserved slides which are available and inexpensive to use.

- **Glassware/plasticware:** With use of glassware in the middle school science laboratory, there is increased risk of glass shattering and students getting cut. The prudent practice is to use plasticware where possible. Should a student get cut, have first-aid materials available such as wipes, sterile gauze pads, and bandages. Try to have the student address his or her own needs to stop the bleeding if possible. The teacher's job is to keep other students away from the area. Depending on the employer's practice, the teacher may help the student, if necessary, but should wear protective gloves as a minimum. Never handle broken glass with an unprotected hand.

- **Sharps:** Have students use extra caution if using utility knives or other sharps while doing laboratory work. Training and demonstrations are the best defense! Never handle a sharp with an unprotected hand.

- **Dried blood:** Use caution when dried blood is discovered in the laboratory. HIV can survive 5-plus days and Hepatitis viruses can survive more than 10 days in dried blood. Most schools have trained custodial help to clean up dried blood. The teacher's job should be to keep others away from it.

- **Vomitus:** Although this happens more often in the elementary school level, students get sick and teachers have been known to be the unintentional recipient of projectile vomitus. Remember that bloodborne pathogens may be transmitted through the mucous membranes of the eyes (tear ducts), nose, and mouth.

- **Physical fighting:** Realistically, teachers are exposed to one or more fights between students during their careers. Use utmost caution in stopping the fight. Do not put yourself in harm's way relative to splashing of blood or biting.

- **Field experiences:** Field experiences are great opportunities for students to work directly in nature's laboratory. However, precautions and preparations must be taken to protect students and science teachers from bloodborne pathogen vectors such as ticks and mosquitoes. Long pants, long-sleeved shirts, hats, and so on, should be worn to protect again ticks and mosquito bites. Also, checking after the field trip for these insects on clothing and skin is a prudent practice.

If any blood or potential blood product gets on clothing, the clothing should be removed and placed in a biohazard regulated waste bag for proper disposal. Teachers may decide to have their clothing laundered. If this is the case, the employer is normally responsible for the cost, providing the incident occurred at the worksite.

Any exposure incident should be treated immediately by first washing the exposed areas with soap and water. In the meantime secure the assistance of the school medical support person. Also be familiar with the basic first aid response in the school's bloodborne pathogen plan. Students should also be trained as part of the prelaboratory primer. No matter how large or small, report any suspected exposures to the school medical support person!

Resources

Centers for Disease Control

- Lyme disease—*www.cdcgov/ncidod/dvbid/lyme/index.htm*

- Bloodborne pathogens—*www.cdc.gov/niosh/topics/bbp*

- Hepatitis—*www.cdc.gov/ncidod/diseases/hepatitis/index.htm*

Kwan, T., and J. Texley. 2002. *Inquiring safely: A guide for middle school teachers.* Arlington, VA: NSTA Press.

OSHA Bloodborne Pathogen Standards—*www.osha.gov/SLTC/bloodbornepathogens/standards.html*

SECTION

III

**SAFETY IN
SCIENCE INSTRUCTION**

25. Demonstration Safety

The National Science Education Standards foster hands-on, process- and inquiry-based science (NRC 1996). This equates to more laboratory work for students and more demonstrations for science teachers. Demonstrations give teachers a chance to present discrepant events and other attention-grabbing phenomena that make an impression on students. Many of us have vivid memories of light shows, loud noises, projectiles, and other sensory-stimulating events that left us wanting to know more about the science behind the spectacle.

Unfortunately, too many students have vivid memories of demonstrations that went awry. According to statistics, more than 150 students have been seriously injured over the past four years in science laboratories or classrooms, many during demonstrations. One of the more recent accidents occurred at a high school in Illinois. A flame test demonstration turned into an alcohol-fueled fireball and injured more than a half a dozen students. Some of the seriously burned required skin grafts.

When accidents occur, the administration usually responds by imposing a moratorium on demonstrations and lab activities. Imagine if authorities reacted in a similar manner in the real world. Airplanes would no longer fly and cars would no longer be driven. Just as we depend on planes and cars for transportation, science teachers depend on labs and demonstrations to teach effectively. So, the proper response to an accident isn't to ban labs and demonstrations, but to identify the cause of the accident and introduce or enforce safety guidelines for prevention. What contributes to potential safety problems with demonstrations are issues such as overcrowded laboratories and classrooms, outdated and ill-equipped science facilities, lack of teacher and student safety training, poor safety planning, and unenforced safety standards.

Safety Considerations

Given the inherent need for teacher demonstrations in science classrooms and laboratories, the alternative is to safely prepare for success. The following safety strategies should be addressed in considering science demonstrations:

Test run—Test the demonstration before carrying it out in front of a class or audience. This allows you to more safely troubleshoot problems, make modifications, and deal with any surprises.

Planning—Know what protective equipment you will need and have a plan in place for controlling hazardous elements of the demonstration, such as fire and chemicals.

Ventilation—Determine what type of ventilation system will be needed to handle any fumes or smoke. Make sure your fume hood is in good working order if it will be used.

Fire suppression equipment—If flames are involved, check the location and condition of your fire extinguisher and fire emergency blanket.

Eye protection—If hazardous liquids will be used, appropriate eye protection, such as chemical-splash goggles, are required for both students and demonstrators. If necessary, a chemical safety shield should be placed between the demonstration and the audience. If solid projectiles are used, appropriate safety glasses should be used.

Aprons and gloves—If hazardous liquids will be used, students and the demonstrator should wear gloves and aprons.

MSDS—Determine the chemical nature of the demonstration materials (corrosivity, flammability, reactivity, and toxicity).

Consult material safety data sheets and share them with the audience before the demonstration.

Control of energy—Have access to master shutoffs for utilities—gas, electricity, and water. Your students also should know where the controls are located and how they operate.

Inspection—Make sure the area where the demonstration is to take place has been inspected for hazards, such as dangerous chemicals and trip and slip hazards such as wires and spills on the floor. Good housekeeping is critical.

Emergency eyewash and shower—Eyewash stations and acid showers must be available and operational. They must be inspected before demonstrations to make sure they are in working order, especially if hazardous materials will be used.

Evacuation procedures—Be certain that evacuation procedures are established and drilled in case there is need.

Use of hazardous chemicals—Wherever possible, substitute less hazardous chemicals for those with greater hazards. Also, use smaller amounts or less concentrated solutions. Think twice before using hazardous chemicals with students.

Network in advance—Teaching is about sharing ideas and experiences. Knowledge gained from books, the internet, colleagues, and other sources can help make a demonstration successful.

Use of educational technology—If your laboratory or science classroom does not have appropriate engineering and safety equipment, have students watch a videotape of you performing the demonstration.

Work with administrators to bring your laboratory and science classroom up-to-code for the protection of both students and teachers. Certainly, the benefits of demonstrations outweigh the risks. By following safety procedures and training, you will minimize the probability of an incident and the level of risk.

Reference

National Research Council (NRC). 1996. *National Science Education Standards*. Washington, DC: National Academy Press.

26. Check Your Activity Kits

Science activity kits are available from a variety of textbook publishers and science laboratory suppliers, both for elementary and secondary level programs. For some school districts, the convenience, organization, curriculum scope, and sequence provided by these kits make them a tempting choice for incorporating hands-on, process- and inquiry-based science in the classroom.

When teachers consider adopting whole curricular packages or individual kits, they should make sure the safety piece is in place. Questions teachers should address before investing in a kit include the following:

- Are the activities safe?

- Are the activities age appropriate?

- Is personal protective equipment included?

- Are material safety data sheets (MSDSs) provided?

- Can the activity be done safely in a science classroom or science laboratory?

The definition of *safe* has become much more conservative over the last 50 years. Part of the issue is the fact that students today tend to be more physiologically sensitive to allergens. For example, one of the original National Science Foundation kits called for students to raise mold spores with little direction about isolating cultures. Today, many students are mold-allergen sensitive—some at a life-threatening level. At the very minimum, mold culturing should be done only in an isolated environment such as a plastic container with a cover or a closed, sealed petri plate.

Another kit allowed middle school students to handle samples of radioactive ore. Again, what we know today about these products would either prevent use or

require a defined protective casing so students would not directly handle the material. The bottom line is that kit activities should not put students in harm's way.

Age Appropriate

Make sure the activity kits you plan on using are age appropriate. Most suppliers provide this information in their promotional literature. For example, Delta Education provides a full scope and sequence by grade for their SCIS 3+ Program (*www.deltaeducation.com/scisgallery.aspx?collection=N&menuID=11*), indicating which kits are appropriate for particular grade levels. If a kit's description includes no age-level recommendation, be certain to contact the supplier and ask for it. Should that information not be available, move to another supplier!

Personal Protective Equipment

Personal protective equipment (PPE) is an essential part of safety. Kits should provide the PPE students need to carry out their work or specify where it can be secured. For example, if an activity kit calls for vinegar or acetic acid, chemical-splash goggles are required. Using sand paper for sanding balsa wood requires safety glasses or goggles. Use of weights requires closed-toe shoes—no sandals. Again, the student and teacher directions should spell out any safety issues and PPE requirements.

MSDS Availability

MSDS are necessary and required for use of hazardous chemicals by the Occupational Safety and Health Administration (OSHA) as part of the Hazard Communications program and Laboratory Standard. Kits should be supplied with MSDS information for specific hazardous chemicals used in activities. Some suppliers provide this information directly online. For example, at Carolina Biological's website (*www.*

carolina.com/labsafety/msds/default.asp), teachers can download specific MSDS for items from that site. Other companies, such as Fisher Scientific, provide an MSDS fax-on-demand service that will fax an MSDS directly to your school.

A Safe Environment

The beauty of most activity kits is that they can be done in the science classroom, laboratory, or field. Most are simple in content so as not to require specific laboratory-level engineering controls like ventilation, shower, eyewash, and so on. However, it must be reemphasized that teachers need to be prudent when planning activities. For example, if a hazardous chemical is required, make sure protective eyewear is in place, eyewash facilities are available, and medical support can be summoned immediately.

The Maryland Public Schools Science Safety Manual (*www.mdk12.org/instruction/curriculum/science/safety/index.html*) addresses safety issues in the science classroom and laboratory. The manual notes that teachers and students can avoid accidents by

- using the proper equipment,
- making sure that the equipment is clean and in good working order,

- receiving instruction in the proper use of all equipment, and
- practicing proper use of equipment.

In addition, it notes that laboratories are safest when

- care is taken in selecting and using reagents,
- chemicals are properly labeled and stored,
- student safety is considered when determining an activity's value,
- hazards are anticipated and precautions taken to ensure proper function of equipment,
- safety rules are established and enforced, and
- supervision is provided during all science activities.

Always check out and run through activities in kits before assigning them to students. The extra planning and experience time will make for an even safer environment.

27. Field Trips

Every good field trip requires extra adult help. The number of chaperones isn't set by a formula: It depends upon where you are going, how much you'll expect of your students, and whether special-needs students will be included. Preplanning should take place *with* your chaperones. Unprepared adults can be less than helpful. And the chaperones should never be distracted by the presence of their own children on the trip.

Many field trips involve field studies, like rock collecting or pond analysis. Visit your site in advance. Use your special "teacher eyes" to try to anticipate the worst that might happen. Is there something that shouldn't be climbed—but might be, such as a high-tension wire? Are there water, poison ivy, polluted water? Do you have permission to use all the property areas you need?

Take With You

Packing light is probably not the best advice for school field trips. As you leave the support of your institution, you'll be principal, teacher, and guide. You'll enjoy that trip all the more knowing you've made every precaution for safety. Here are a few essentials:

- Reviewing your board of education's field trip policy.

- Information about your students' medical needs, allergies, and contact information. You must know about special needs and have written permission to obtain help for your students if the worst takes place.

- Directions and material safety date sheets (MSDSs). If your trip involves use of laboratory chemicals of any kind, you must bring both. Take only the minimum amount of chemicals in a locked container. In general, whenever you can avoid carrying test chemicals on a field trip, leave them at home. Also, instead of using chemicals in the field to perform tests, you might use portable probes.

- A cell phone or two-way, long-range walkie-talkie that will keep you in touch with the school. You'll need one for emergencies and to let the school know when you'll be arriving back so that parents can meet you.

- Appropriate dress and repellents for insects. West Nile and other insect-borne diseases are serious threats in many areas now. Make sure that you've informed parents in advance about the use of repellants, so that potential allergic reactions can be avoided.

- Behavior contracts with consequences that everyone understands and supports.

Don't Bring

- Siblings or friends—other children who will not be subject to the rules you have set up.

- Student cell phones, extra games, very loud audio equipment, or materials that could distract or be stolen.

28. Plan for Guests

Guest speakers can motivate students and help them understand real-world science. Physicians discussing heart transplants, police inspectors talking about forensics, and engineers explaining building airplanes bring science alive for students. Members of the community are often willing to donate their time for a day to work with students, bringing with them a wealth of knowledge, cutting-edge technology, and exciting, everyday applications of science concepts. Contact colleagues, parents, your chamber of commerce, local colleges, and other resources for guest speakers. Getting parents involved is especially rewarding and can provide you with valuable support for your science program.

However, teachers need to take steps to maximize the benefits of having a guest speaker. Most presenters do not necessarily have the teaching skills needed to make a meaningful and safe presentation for students without the helping and planning of the teacher. Below are a number of steps that teachers can take to better prepare the speaker and the students for a safe and successful experience.

Guest Speaker Strategy and Planning List

Let the students know that they are having a guest speaker. Review the expectations for behavior and safety with them and make clear the consequences of failing to follow the guidelines.

Determine if there are board of education or school policies for having guest speakers in your classroom. Read and follow any district or school practices.

Inform the principal's office about your plans for having a guest speaker, and give staff the schedule and specifics of the presentation. Invite the building administrators, science department supervisor, and colleagues to the presentation.

Develop a speaker information folder that sets the expectations for the guest speaker and provides information for a successful program. Include in the folder such items as

- relevant school board policies on guest speakers;

- appropriate literature;

- controls on hazardous material use, projectiles, firearms, and controlled substances;

- request for educational technology needs (computer, LCD projector, VCR);

- confirmation of date and time for presentation;

- directions to school;

- security procedures;

- parking instructions; and

- safety regulations and procedures, such as information on personnel protective equipment, hazardous chemical use, and evacuation plans.

Review safety regulations and procedures, including your school's chemical hygiene plan, with the guest speaker. Have the speaker write a basic lesson plan in advance for approval if activities, experiments, or demonstrations will be done. This is especially crucial if hazardous chemicals will be used. Review the plan for appropriateness and safety, and approve any changes in the plan before the presentation. As a licensed professional and employee, a teacher carries the bulk of the responsibility in this case. Also have a letter of agreement that is signed by both the science teacher and the presenter, acknowledging the plan and expectations to follow.

Design student feedback forms for the presenter. Have student and teacher evaluation forms completed and summaries shared with the speaker. Teachers should read the forms before they are returned to the speaker and edit out any offensive or inappropriate comments.

Student feedback forms could include items such as

- usefulness of information presented;
- level of interest in topic;
- relevance to area of study; and
- general comments and recommendations.

A teacher feedback form could include items such as

- grade appropriateness;
- areas of strength;
- areas of least interest; and
- general comments and suggestions.

A speaker feedback form to be given to the teacher could include

- availability and operation of educational technology;
- communications and arrangements;
- specific expertise;
- future interest in presenting; and
- general recommendations.

Always follow up with a thank-you note. Guest speakers especially enjoy cards or notes from students.

29. Model and Project Guidelines

Each year Richard Broggini, an eighth-grade science teacher at Smith Middle School in Glastonbury, Connecticut, has had his students do unusual projects. The first assignment he developed required a class of life science students to create full-scale human skeleton models from recycled or reusable materials. Students used plastic milk bottles for heads, thread spools for foot bones, and other common items to complete the skeleton. Realizing that some of the recycled materials could be hazardous, Richard developed strict guidelines governing what materials could be used. Before the skeleton construction began, each team of builders had to submit a list of materials for approval.

For a subsequent project in Earth science, he asked students to build life-size alien models adapted to the characteristics of a particular planet's atmosphere and land features. As part of a physical science unit, his students built solar cookers out of recycled materials. Again, with each of these model assignments, materials and designs are reviewed and approved before building begins.

Guidelines

If you are like Richard and enjoy having your students engage in model building and other hands-on projects, I offer the following basic safety guidelines:

- Document safety precautions and guidelines to protect yourself.

- Remind students of appropriate laboratory behavior and consequences for failing to obey them.

- Define expectations and limitations and prescribe guidelines for students. They need to know the purpose of the project or model they are building and what is acceptable and unacceptable during the construction process.

- Set up a review process for each student to secure your approval prior to the construction phase, such as the purpose of model, diagram of model, materials, and safety precautions.

- Be certain to weigh the educational value against the risks associated with any model or project.

- Model any safety behaviors for students—for example, lighting a Bunsen burner, pouring liquids, and using a hot glue gun.

- Make sure students know the hazards associated with the materials, processes, and equipment they will be using. Material safety data sheets (MSDSs) may be helpful in this area.

- Review the location and proper use of protective equipment such as safety glasses or goggles, gloves, aprons, emergency shower, eyewash, and fire extinguisher.

- Review with students how to respond to an emergency, such as small fire or hazardous chemical spill.

- Check that adequate ventilation is available to accommodate vapors and gases being produced in the laboratory. Look for indicators of improper ventilation—such as headache, runny eyes and nose, and sore throat—among students.

- Keep areas clean and uncluttered to prevent trip and fall hazards. Provide students with storage bags or boxes to keep their personal items in until the end of class.

- Require students to quickly wipe up any spills.

- Do not allow food or drink in the classroom and have students wash their hands at the end of class.

- Familiarize yourself with students' medical profiles or predispositions that could be compromised, such as allergic reactions to specific materials or chemicals.

- Caution students to make sure their hands are away from the front of any sharp tool or object, and tell them to cut away from the body.

- Use leg and arm muscles, never back muscles, to lift heavy objects.

- Be sure to walk around the laboratory observing the process and providing individual assistance to ensure safety.

- Inform parents about special project or model building so they can be supportive and helpful. Parents can also be recruited to help with project work—especially if they have background in carpentry, science, crafts, or another useful skill—and to serve as another pair of eyes and hands.

30. Think "Occupant Load"

What is the safest number of students for one teacher to teach? Like many issues in education, there is no one-size-fits-all answer. Several factors need to be considered when establishing the safest number of students. First of all, forget the phrase *class size*. *Occupant load* is the more appropriate legal term, and is used in codes published by the National Fire Protection Association (NFPA), the Building Officials and Code Administrators (BOCA), and the International Code Council (ICC). (Check with your local fire marshal for a free copy of these codes.) The use of the instructional space must also be considered. Will the space be used as a classroom or laboratory? Certainly, the laboratory is a much more dangerous place, which would be reflected in the occupancy load.

Professional Standards

Professional standards fall into the quasi-legal realm. For example, the 1990 NSTA (National Science Teachers Assocation) Board of Directors adopted a position statement, Laboratory Science, that recommends that the number of students assigned to each middle school laboratory class should not exceed 24. The student must have immediate access to the teacher in order to provide a safe and effective learning environment."A more recent NSTA position statement, Safety and School Science Instruction, recommends that the maximum number of occupants in a laboratory teaching space be based on the

- building and fire safety codes,

- occupancy load limits,

- design of the laboratory teaching facility, and

- supervision needs of students (see Resources).

The Laboratory Science statement reflects more of an academic standard than a safety standard. It really says that the optimal class size for meeting the academic needs of students should not exceed 24 students per instructor. However, it is Safety and School Science Instruction that really addresses the class size or occupancy load question. For example, although Laboratory Science recommends that the class size not exceed 24, Safety and School Science Instruction recommends that the occupancy load should be considerably smaller if the laboratory is smaller than 1,000 square feet. The position statements are designed to work in concert with each other, not alone (see Resources).

Legal Standards

Safety and School Science Instruction references building and fire safety codes, along with occupancy load limits. Middle school science laboratories are classified as laboratories by safety standards set by NFPA, BOCA, and/or ICC and the Occupational Safety and Health Administration (OSHA). Occupancy loads establish the load factor. For example, educational occupancies are set at 50 net square feet per occupant. However, the laboratory must be analyzed to determine the actual design load that will permit occupants to exit safely in case of an emergency. Factors such as the type and location of laboratory furniture, utilities, hazardous chemicals used, sprinkler systems, and number of exits are considered in determining the occupancy load level. The authority having local jurisdiction, such as the town fire marshal, (e.g., town fire marshal) determines the occupancy load for science laboratories.

Handling Overcrowding?

Overloaded classes are a serious issue. The problem is that if a licensed professional—

a.k.a., the teacher)—knowingly has students occupy an overloaded laboratory and an accident occurs, there could be liability issues. To avoid such situations, teachers should consider a number of strategies.

- Determine the occupancy load levels for science laboratories and classrooms. Again, the local fire marshal can be helpful. Secure these findings in writing.

- Share overloaded class issues and findings with department and building supervisors and administrators in writing. Explore and suggest options for reducing overloaded class sizes. (See Section IV: Questions From Teachers, 11. Overcrowded Labs, p. 112.)

- Make the point that the National Science Education Standards and most state science frameworks foster hands-on inquiry and process-oriented instructional experiences for middle school. However, if overloaded classes are an issue, consideration must be given to limiting or even aborting laboratory work until the occupancy standard is met, for safety and liability reasons.

- Make use of local bargaining agents such as teacher unions and associations that can be helpful in advocating for a safe working environment. Contact union stewards or association representatives to determine how they can be of support.

If these suggestions fail, you can contact the insurer for the school district to request an inspection. Another option is to submit a complaint to OSHA or a similar occupational safety office in the state. Understand that OSHA does not address student safety. However, as an employee, your safety may be at stake as a result of overcrowding in a laboratory. Also, you can check to see if teachers at your school have liability insurance at the local, district, and state level. Consider securing individual professional liability insurance if overcrowding and other unsafe conditions persist at your school.

The easiest way to work with supervisors and administrators is to educate them. In most cases they are not the enemy, but allies in fostering the educational process and learning environment. They often have constraints placed on them that stand in the way of resolving important issues. Help them understand that science is different from other disciplines. Hopefully, there will be common ground from which solutions can be launched. Be patient, but also be safe in what is done.

Resources

Kwan, T., and J. Texley. 2002. *Inquiring safely: A guide for middle school teachers*. Arlington, VA: NSTA.

NSTA Position Statement: The Integral Role of Laboratory Investigations in Science Instruction—*www.nsta.org/about/positions/laboratory.aspx*.

NSTA Position Statement: Safety and School Science Instruction—*www.nsta.org/about/positions/safety.aspx*.

Ryan, K. 2001. *Science classroom safety and the law, a handbook for teachers*. Batavia, IL: Flinn Scientific.

31. Special-Needs Students

With the advent of inclusion legislation such as the Individuals with Disabilities Education Act (IDEA) or PL 105-17 Reauthorization Action of 1997, many schools have focused on teaching partnerships between regular education and special-needs education teachers. Science departments have been no exception to the trend toward team teaching. Sharon A. Maroney, associate professor of special education at Western Illinois University, has identified five of the most popular models of team teaching (see Resources, Some Notes on Team Teaching):

Traditional Team Teaching—Both teachers are involved in sharing instruction for content and skills for all students. In this format, both teachers accept equal responsibility for the education of all students and are involved throughout the class period. Science teachers and special education teachers tend to adopt this model after several years of working together. Once comfort levels are raised, this approach is often chosen.

Complementary or supportive instruction—One teacher assumes the responsibility for teaching the content while the other teacher provides follow-up instructional activities on related topics or study skills.

Parallel instruction—The class is divided into two groups, and each receives instruction on the same content or skills from one of the two teachers.

Differentiated split class—The class is divided into two groups according to students' specified learning needs. Each group is provided with instruction to meet a specified need.

Monitoring teacher—One teacher assumes the responsibility for classroom instruction while the other teacher moves about the room and monitors student work and behavior. The monitoring-teacher model is popular in science labs because it allows the science teacher to deliver the lesson using his or her expertise, while the special education teacher moves around the lab to observe and assist individual students. Once the special education and science teachers are comfortable in their roles, they can switch responsibilities on an alternating basis.

Legal Issues

Early federal law did not require the inclusion of all students with disabilities into the regular classroom. With the implementation of legislation such as PL 94-142 in 1975, the phrase *least restrictive environment* came into play. This translated into most special-needs students being placed and accommodated in mainstream classrooms rather than being restricted in self-contained special-education classrooms. Updated legislation in the late 1990s, however, made alternative placement the exception, not the rule. Except in extreme cases where an alternative placement is determined by an individualized education program (IEP) or by action of a planning and placement team (PPT), most students are mainstreamed. At this time, placement of a student is based on a school's justifying why the student should be excluded as opposed to parents' justifying why a child should be included.

With the advent of IDEA, least-restrictive environment issues were broadened to include instruction conducted in the classroom, clubs, athletics, and other learning environments. Legal criteria have been established to help determine least restrictive environment placements. For example, summarized reports of Osborne and Dimattia (1994) and Martin (1994) defined factors in least-restrictive environment legal decisions. Those factors and conclusions included the following

- Not all children with disabilities are required to be placed in the general education environment.

- Children with disabilities may not be excluded because the school finds it less difficult to educate the child in a segregated classroom.

- The fact that a child cannot keep pace with peers in general education is not justification for exclusion.

- The fact that curriculum modification puts a burden on the classroom teacher is not justification for exclusion.

- Social benefits from participating in general education may be of equal importance to academic training.

- Children whose behavior impairs the learning of other students may be excluded, but attempts to address the problem, such as training of the teacher or different management of the child, may first have to be demonstrated to be unsuccessful.

- Excessive costs of "supplementary aids and services" to accommodate a child in the mainstream may be reason to justify exclusion.

The bottom line is that students may be removed from the regular education classroom only if the disability makes it impossible for education to occur in the regular classroom despite use of supplementary aids and services.

Collaboration and Safety Issues

A number of issues must be addressed by science teachers working with children having disabilities in both team-taught and non-team-taught classes. These issues are

The safety of students and/or teacher (employee)—The Occupational Safety and Health Administration's (OSHA)

Laboratory Standard (29 CFR 1910.1450) requires a safe working environment for employees. Criteria for achieving this environment are addressed in the school's chemical hygiene plan (CHP). Science teachers should make sure their department's CHP includes a statement such as, "In order to secure a safe working environment for employees in the laboratory, all occupants (including students) are to follow prudent laboratory practices and procedures." This statement clarifies what is acceptable behavior for all occupants.

The safety of students needing assistance—An actual case best illustrates this concern. A legally blind student was placed into a 10th-grade chemistry course. After a few weeks, the instructor expressed concern to the administration about the safety of the blind student and other occupants in the chemistry laboratory. The State Department of Education sent a student advocate to a planning and placement team (PPT) meeting requested by the administration and teacher. The advocate wanted the student to have unrestricted movement in the laboratory without the assistance of an aide or support person. The teacher again noted her concern relative to all occupants' safety, especially given the dangers inherent in the laboratory, such as acids and Bunsen burners.

Ultimately, the school's safety compliance officer required that the district provide an in-the-laboratory special aide to help the blind student in laboratory work. The compliance officer made this decision based on the OSHA requirement for a safe employee working environment noted in the CHP. Also addressed was the board of education's policy on providing a safe learning environment for students. The aide was provided and the blind student successfully completed the course without incident.

The need for appropriate equipment—The Americans with Disabilities Act prescribes specifications relative to access for equipment such as sinks, eyewash stations, and desks. It is critical from a safety standpoint that these specifications be met for all students to have a safe laboratory experience.

The number of occupants in the laboratory—Many teachers believe that class inclusion of special-needs students requires smaller class sizes. Believe it or not, research evidence currently suggests that class size has little effect on achievement. However, research evidence does suggest that class size has an effect on safety. Both OSHA and BOCA (Building Officials and Code Administrators) and/or ICC (International Code Council) limit laboratory occupancy loads to secure a safe working environment. In the case of special-needs students, the aide is considered another occupant and must be figured into the occupancy load.

The liability involved in team teaching—If a science teacher collaboratively teaches a science class with a special education teacher (holding only special education certification), who has the liability for the safety of students? Given that both teachers are state licensed, there is shared liability for maintaining general student safety. However, in issues dealing with specific safety situations for science laboratory operations, the shared liability would not be considered equal. It is critical that special education teachers in laboratory-based, team-teaching situations receive the same safety training provided the science teacher. This shows good faith in efforts to foster a safe working environment for students and employees.

Inclusion can be a wonderful thing both academically and socially for students with special needs and their classmates. On the other hand, special attention must be given to safety issues and training to maintain a safe working environment for all.

References

Martin, R. 1994. What the courts have said about inclusion. *LDA/Newsbriefs* May/June: 22–25.

Osborne, A.G., and P. Dimattia. 1994. The IDEA's least restrictive environment mandate: Legal implications. *Exceptional Children* 61: 6–14.

Internet Resources

Some Notes on Team Teaching—*www.wiu. edu/users/mfsam1/TeamTchg.html*

Teaching science to students with special needs—*www.as.wvu.edu/~scidis*

Writing a chemical hygiene plan—*www.osha. gov/SLTC/laboratories/index.html*

32. Green Chemistry

One easy way to reduce the number of accidents in your lab is to go green. Green chemistry, or sustainable chemistry, emerged about a decade ago, but the concept has been practiced for centuries by indigenous people of many continents. The basic principles of green chemistry are that you should use only what you need and recycle what you can.

Paul T. Anastas, an organic chemist working in the Office of Pollution Prevention and Toxins at EPA, coined the term green chemistry in 1991. It was defined as "the utilization of a set of principles that reduces or eliminates the use or generation of hazardous substances in the design, manufacture, and application of chemical products." Since that time, the definition has been expanded to include the production or use of improved chemicals with less waste, less energy, and reduced environmental impacts. Green chemistry also seeks to foster safer reactions by substituting nonhazardous chemicals for those that pose high risks, thereby reducing the quantities of hazardous chemical waste.

Green Labs are Safer

Microchemistry—using small amounts of chemicals instead of the large amounts called for in traditional labs—is an important part of green chemistry. However, green chemistry also requires that you

- create less-hazardous waste chemicals;
- store fewer hazardous waste chemicals;
- expose humans and the environment to little or no toxic chemicals;
- avoid unsafe solvents;
- stop creating chemical products that, when disposed of, will remain in the environment for long periods of time; and
- desist from using chemicals that have the potential for laboratory accidents, such as fires and explosions.

These goals reflect the Twelve Principles of Green Chemistry, the bedrock upon which the green chemistry movement is grounded (see box, next page).

Greening a Lab

You can begin converting a conventional science laboratory to a green laboratory in a number of ways. For existing science laboratories, use the following strategies:

- Plan hands-on science labs and activities that use environmentally friendly chemicals in lieu of environmentally unfriendly chemicals. In other words, use chemicals that can easily be recycled and have little or no impact on the environment. For example, using commercial vinegar in place of hydrochloric or sulfuric acids is a start. Greener chemicals also tend to be less expensive.

- Order only those chemicals that you will need for one year instead of larger amounts that may never be used. This requires less space and a lower level of maintenance. Keeping your chemical inventory up-to-date can help you achieve this goal.

- Use only small amounts of chemicals based on microscale methods and apparatus. In other words, instead of using grams of chemicals, use centigrams.

- Alternative computer simulations of laboratories that require no chemicals can be infused into certain sections of the science course.

- Make use of laboratory hoods when possible to reduce the volume use of general ventilation in the laboratory. This can save on heating or cooling energy if the laboratory has variable damper controls.

- Stress the connection between green chemistry and the environment by modeling green activities in the laboratory. Sustainable development is key to the future.

When renovating or building new laboratories, the following strategies can be implemented:

- Design laboratory ventilation in ways that are within the fire code but also green friendly. For example, hoods can be used for certain experiments if necessary in lieu of increasing the ventilation in the whole laboratory.

- Select time-tested, milled-wood laboratory furniture that will stand up to use and abuse over time.

- Design laboratories to make use of active and/or passive solar energy, photovoltaic

Twelve principles of green chemistry

Prevention—It is better to prevent waste than to treat or clean up waste after it has been created.

Atom economy—Synthetic methods should be designed to maximize the incorporation of all materials used in the process into the final product.

Less-hazardous chemical syntheses—Wherever practical, synthetic methods should be designed to use and generate substances that possess little or no toxicity to human health and the environment.

Design safer chemicals—Chemical products should be designed to effect their desired function while minimizing their toxicity.

Safer solvents and auxiliaries—The use of auxiliary substances—solvents, separation agents, and others—should be made unnecessary wherever possible and innocuous when used.

Design for energy efficiency—Energy requirements of chemical processes should be recognized for their environmental and economic impacts and should be minimized. If possible, synthetic methods should be conducted at ambient temperature and pressure.

Use renewable feedstocks—A raw material or feedstock should be renewable rather than depleting whenever technically and economically practicable.

Reduce derivatives—Unnecessary derivatives, such as the use of blocking groups, protection and deprotection, and temporary modification of physical and chemical processes, should be minimized or avoided because such steps require additional reagents and can generate waste.

Catalysis—Catalytic reagents (as selective as possible) are superior to stoichiometric reagents.

Design for degradation—Chemical products should be designed so that at the end of their function they break down into innocuous degradation products and do not persist in the environment.

Real-time analysis for pollution prevention—Analytical methodologies need to be further developed to allow for real-time, in-process monitoring and control prior to the formation of hazardous substances.

Inherently safer chemistry for accident prevention—Substances and the form of a substance used in a chemical process should be chosen to minimize the potential for chemical accidents, including releases, explosions, and fires.

technology, heat pumps, and the myriad other alternative energy sources available. This also includes such basic steps as proper insulation and window fixings.

- Use natural lighting whenever possible.

- Design laboratory utilities that reduce volume use. For example, have water restriction valves on lab benches to save water.

- Use recyclable labware whenever possible.

- Design laboratory waste retrieval or neutralizing technology, such as an acid trap, to render select chemicals going down the drain harmless to the environment.

Reference

Anastas, P. T., and J. C. Warner, eds. 1998. *Green chemistry: Theory and practice*. New York: Oxford University Press.

Internet Resources

ACS Green Chemistry website—*www.chemistry. org/education/greenchem*

EPA's Green Chemistry Program—*www.epa. gov/greenchemistry*

EPA Green Chemistry Institute Listserv—*gci-list@acs.org*

Greening Schools—*www.greeningschools.org*

National Clearinghouse for Educational Facilities—*www.edfacilities.org/rl/science.cfm*

Royal Society of Chemistry's Green Chemistry Network—*www.chemsoc.org/networkds/gen/index.htm*

33. Safer Electricity

Lighting a fluorescent bulb by touching it to the nose of a student who has one hand on an electrostatic generator is an illuminating demonstration of the properties of voltage. It demonstrates that the several hundred thousand volts of electricity passing through the student's body are not dangerous. But students and teachers need to understand that the current running through a circuit does pose a real danger.

According to Ohms Law, $E = IR$ (where E equals the electromotive force, I the amperage or current, and R the resistance), as resistance decreases, current increases. For example, dry skin has high resistance to electron flow, causing dissipation of energy, mostly in the form of heat. Wet skin can reduce the amount of Ohms (the unit of resistance) about 500,000 times. Consequently, touching a live wire with a dry hand may result in only a burn while touching it with a wet hand can result in electrocution. The amount of current or amperage affects the severity of the shock.

In the fluorescent bulb demonstration, the approximately 100 microamps flowing through the student's body create a mild tingling sensation. Amperage exceeding approximately 10 milliamps, however, can produce a severe shock. Current surpassing 200 milliamps is potentially fatal.

Electrical shock not only produces heat that can burn tissue, but it can also overload the nervous system's circuitry and cause involuntary muscle contractions. In severe cases, contraction of the diaphragm and heart muscles can interfere with breathing and heart rhythms.

A Battery of Safe Practices

The study of electricity can be fun and exciting at the middle school level if the following safety guidelines are followed:

- Be sure all laboratory circuits are under the control of a master cut-off switch with easy access from any location in a room.

- Do not let anyone touch a grounded utility, such as a gas or water pipe, and an electrical circuit at the same time.

- Do not store flammable liquids near electrical equipment because of the potential for fire and explosion.

- Remind students that the human body is a conductor of electricity.

- Review the proper procedure for disengaging someone who is being shocked. Inform students that they should never directly touch a person who is being shocked, but make contact with a nonconductor such as rubber instead.

- Inspect three-pronged, grounded plugs for damage before using them.

- Inspect all wire insulation to make sure it is intact and not worn or frayed.

- Be sure all laboratory circuits have ground-fault interrupters, or GFCI, protection.

- Never work with electrical equipment using wet hands or when standing in wet areas.

- Approved carpeting, rubber mats, or wood floors are best when working with electricity.

- Electrical equipment should be plugged directly into wall receptacles. Extension cords are only for temporary use. Remember that they are trip hazards and when heated up can cause fires. They also may overload a circuit.

- Electrical cords should be removed from wall receptacles by pulling the plug only, not the cord.

- All electrical appliances and power tools should be properly grounded with a three-pronged plug before and during use to prevent electrocution.

- Use tools with nonconducting handles when working on electrical circuits during activities.

- Advise students not to do experiments with electric circuits at home or school except under the direct supervision of an adult.

- Batteries (1.5 volts) are safe unless they are short-circuited, become overheated, and explode, which can cause serious burns to the body. Never short-circuit a battery.

- When wiring circuits, always place the switch in last or live plug-in. The instructor, prior to power flow, should inspect all circuits.

- When charging capacitors, do not exceed the designed capacitance printed on the device. Also, respect the polarity of capacitors in a fluctuating D/C circuit by making sure the poles are never reversed because improper polarity can cause explosion of the capacitor.

Electricity is all around us. Students need to understand how it can improve as well as endanger life. Learning to respect electricity is the first line of defense in using its power wisely.

34. Laser Pointers

With the introduction of physics concepts at the elementary and middle school grades resulting from the National Science Education Standards and No Child Left Behind legislation, teachers are looking for exciting technology that will turn kids on to the study of light. Enter the laser diode pointer. Given their easy availability, low cost, portability, and inexpensive upkeep (they operate on AAA batteries), laser pointers would seem to be the ideal piece of classroom science equipment. However, before adopting laser pointers for demonstrations or hands-on labs, teachers and students should be aware of the risks associated with their use.

The potential eye hazard is considered limited for unprotected eyes because of the human body's blink reflex to bright light. The reflex time of 0.25 seconds usually limits the exposure. However, this reflex is only effective in clearly visible red to green wavelengths. It is less effective for laser pointers using deep-red wavelengths and totally ineffective for ultraviolet or infrared laser pointers. Therefore, any Class 3A laser emitting nonvisible radiation has no place safety-wise in schools.

Not all laser pointers are made in the United States, so not all of those that find their way into classrooms meet American National Standards Institute (ANSI) expectations. More powerful laser pointers are available from Russian and Chinese distributors that often lack proper certification or labeling. For example, one imported laser was found to operate at 532 nm, which equates to a power of about 0.85 mW. Another imported laser pointer was found to emit a 5 mW beam. It had no labeling and the 1064 nm blocking filter was easily removed, which resulted in a beam that exceeded 15 mW. Both of these violated the standards set forth for laser pointers established by the ANSI.

A further concern is the availability of high-power Class 3B lasers that can exceed 200 mW of power. These lasers have a range of up to 60 miles, and the beams can burst balloons and melt plastic. Students and teachers exposed to these types of laser pointers can experience temporary or more serious eye injury, and other physical damage. Needless to say, this class of laser should never be used in the middle level classroom.

Safety for Pointers

At the middle school level, laser pointers should be used only for demonstration purposes by the teacher, and students should not be allowed to handle the devices. The following are examples of other safety rules for laser pointers, in this case recommended by Rockwell Laser Industries (see Resources):

- Never point a laser pointer of any power at anybody. Pointers should be used to point out or emphasize inanimate objects such as slide images or laboratory apparatus.

- Avoid mirrorlike targets and never stare into a pointer.

- Also, never view a laser beam using an optical instrument, such as a microscope or binoculars.

- Always use the lowest power rating possible and highest divergence where possible. No laser pointer rated at a Class 3B should be used without special provision.

- Laser pointers are not toys and should not be used by young students. It is recommended that the batteries be taken out of the pointer when it is not in use.

- It may be prudent to require facility registration of these devices in order to impress the need for safety awareness.

- Safety personnel and pointer users should be aware that wavelengths around 400–500 nm can cause biological effects of a photobiological nature (e.g., like sunburn).

- Laser pointers above 5 mW should never be used.

- All personnel using a Class 3A laser (including laser pointers) should receive laser safety training from a qualified instructor.

What the FDA Says

In 1997, the Food and Drug Administration (FDA) issued a warning on the misuse of laser pointers. It specifically warned school officials about the possibility of eye damage to students from handheld laser pointers. Although the laser pointers are generally safe for teacher use as a screen or chart highlighter, the availability and use of inferior quality laser pointers by students is a concern.

Laser pointers are not toys. They are useful tools for adults that should only be used by students under careful adult supervision. Lasers should never be directed at the eyes. Misuse of a laser can result in temporary blindness or a more serious eye injury.

The FDA goes on to say that "light energy from a laser pointer aimed into the eye can be more damaging than staring directly into the Sun. This is why federal law requires warning labels on laser products about the danger of exposing the eyes to laser radiation. Momentary exposure, as from an unintentional sweep of laser light across a person's eyes, causes only temporary flash blindness. Flash blindness is a temporary loss of vision that occurs when the eye is suddenly exposed to intense light. This effect can last for several seconds to several minutes. But even this can be dangerous to someone who is driving or performing some other activity for which vision is critical."

At the middle level, it is recommended that laser pointers only be used as part of teacher demonstrations. If your school safety policy permits students to use the devices as part of a hands-on investigation, strict supervision is essential.

Internet Resources

Safety recommendations for use of laser pointers—*www.rli.com/resources/pointer.asp*

Vanderbilt University laser safety manual—*http://frontweb.vuse.vanderbilt.edu/vuse_web/facstaff/VUSE_Laser_Safety.pdf*

35. Model Rocketry

Model rocketry is one of the best ways to get students interested in the physical sciences. Following safety guidelines, rocketry can really turn students on to science and also help them understand the applications of the theories and scientific principles—such as Newton's laws of motion, force, mass, and projectile motion—they are learning. The study and use of rocketry provides a hands-on, process- and inquiry-based science experience. It presents problem-solving approaches for students at all levels.

In 1954, Orville Carlisle designed the first model rocket and rocket engine. As a licensed pyrotechnics expert, Orville, with his brother Robert, designed a rocket and engine for use in lectures on the principles of rocket-powered flight.

With the advent of the Space Age in the 1950s, interest in flight, rockets, and space skyrocketed. Space enthusiasts tried to design, build, and fly rockets as a result of this public interest. Unfortunately, this became a very dangerous activity because hobbyists were using metal parts to craft rockets and dangerous chemicals to make engines. Many enthusiasts were injured or killed when rockets blew up.

Orville believed his designs could solve the safety problems and sent samples to G. Harry Stine, a range safety officer at the White Sands Missile Range. Stine in turn built and flew Orville's models with much success. He then crafted a safety code for model rocketry building.

Before starting rocketry activities and instruction, review local and state regulations. Some states have statutes prescribing types of rockets, locations for launches, and other relevant information. One such resource is Connecticut state law on rocketry, which can be used if a state lacks its own standard. Local ordinances and school policy should also be reviewed. The fire code put out by the National Fire Protection Association also provides valuable guidance. (See Resources for more information on these codes and laws.)

The NAR Model Rocket Safety Code

The National Association of Rocketry (NAR) is the oldest and largest sport rocketry organization in the world. It was established in 1957 and has a membership of more than 80,000 hobbyists. The following is the NAR Model Rocket Safety Code (reprinted with permission from the NAR):

Motors: I will use only commercially made, NAR-certified model rocket motors in the manner recommended by the manufacturer. I will not alter the model rocket motor, its parts, or ingredients in any way.

Recovery: I will always use a recovery system in my model rocket that will return it safely to the ground so that it may be flown again. I will use only flame-resistant recovery wadding if wadding is required by the design of my model rocket.

Weight and power limits: My model rocket will weigh no more than 1,500 grams (53 ounces) at liftoff and its rocket motors will produce no more than 320 Newton-seconds (71.9 pound-seconds) of total impulse. My model rocket will weigh no more than the motor manufacturer's recommended maximum liftoff weight for the motors used, or I will use motors recommended by the manufacturer for my model rocket.

Stability: I will check the stability of my model rocket before its first flight, except when launching a model rocket of already proven stability.

Payloads: My model rocket will never carry live animals (except insects) or a payload intended to be flammable, explosive, or harmful.

Launch site: I will launch my model rocket outdoors in a cleared area, free of tall trees, power lines, buildings, and dry brush and grass. My launch area will be at least as large as that recommended in the accompanying table (below).

Launcher: I will launch my model rocket from a stable launch device that provides rigid guidance until the model rocket has reached a speed adequate to ensure a safe flight path. To prevent accidental eye injury, I will always place the launcher so that the end of the rod is above eye level or I will cap the end of the rod when approaching it. I will cap or disassemble my launch rod when not in use and I will never store it in an upright position. My launcher will have a jet deflector device to prevent the motor exhaust from hitting the ground directly. I will always clear the area around my launch device of brown grass, dry weeds, or other easy-to-burn materials.

Ignition system: The system I use to launch my model rocket will be remotely controlled and electrically operated. It will contain a launching switch that will return to "off" when released. The system will contain a removable safety interlock in series with the launch switch. All persons will remain at least 5 meters (15 feet) from the model rocket when I am igniting motors totaling 30 Newton-seconds or less of total impulse and at least 9 meters (30 feet) from the model rocket when I am igniting motors totaling more than 30 Newton-seconds total impulse. I will use only electrical

igniters recommended by the motor manufacturer that will ignite model rocket motors within one second of the actuation of the launching switch.

Launch safety: I will ensure that people in the launch area are aware of the pending model rocket launch and can see the model rocket's liftoff before I begin my audible five-second countdown. I will not launch my model rocket so its flight path will carry it against a target. If my model rocket suffers a misfire, I will not allow anyone to approach it or the launcher until I have made certain that the safety interlock has been removed or that the battery has been disconnected from the ignition system. I will wait one minute after a misfire before allowing anyone to approach the launcher.

Flying conditions: I will launch my model rocket only when the wind is less than 32 kph (20 mph). I will not launch my model rocket so it flies into clouds, near aircraft in flight, or in a manner that is hazardous to people or property.

Prelaunch test: When conducting research activities with unproven model rocket designs or methods, I will, when possible, determine the reliability of my model rocket by prelaunch tests. I will conduct launching of an unproven design in complete isolation from persons not participating in the actual launching.

Launch angle: My launch device will

Launch site dimensions.			
Installed total impulse (Newton-seconds)	Equivalent motor type	Minimum site dimensions	
		square feet	square meters
0.00–1.25	1/4A, 1/2A	50	15
1.26–2.50	A	100	30
2.51–5.00	B	200	60
5.01–10.00	C	400	120
10.01–20.00	D	500	150
20.01–40.00	E	1,000	300
40.01–80.00	F	1,000	300
80.01–160.00	G	1,000	300
160.01–320.00	2 Gs	1,500	450

be pointed within 30 degrees of the vertical. I will never use model rocket motors to propel any device horizontally.

Recovery safety: If a model rocket becomes entangled in a power line or other dangerous place, I will not attempt to retrieve it.

Materials: My model rocket will be made of lightweight materials such as paper, wood, rubber, and plastic suitable for the power used and the performance of my model rocket. I will not use any metal for the nose cone, body, or fins of a model rocket.

Given the rigorous safety code, training, and commitment to model rocketry, it is considered a relatively safe endeavor for middle school science. Rocket engines are premanufactured, as are most of the lightweight model rockets. The manufacturer quantifies rocket engine force using a code. Launch, delivery, and recovery systems also

help to make the activity safe. Instructionally sound model rocketry is a must in getting students motivated and excited about the physical sciences.

Don't forget the safety glasses or goggles as a safety precaution when using rockets! Make it fun and safe at the same time for you and your students.

Resources

Connecticut Model Rocketry Code—*www. state.ct.us/dps/DFEBS/OSFM/regs/modrock. pdf*

Kwan, T., and J. Texley. 2002. *Inquiring safely: A guide for middle school teachers.* Arlington, VA: NSTA Press.

National Association of Rocketry—*www.nar.org*

National Fire Protection Agency Code for Model Rocketry—*www.nfpa.org*

36. Dissection

In June 2005, the NSTA Board of Directors adopted a revised position statement, "Responsible Use of Live Animals and Dissection in the Science Classroom." Under the "Dissection" section, NSTA calls for more research to determine the effectiveness of animal dissection activities and alternatives, and the extent to which these activities should be integrated into the science curriculum. Until research indicates the effectiveness of alternatives to dissection, many teachers will continue including dissections in their classrooms. Those who do must make sure they are addressing related safety issues to ensure a successful learning experience. (See this position statement on p. 137.)

NSTA Recommendations

The position statement further notes that NSTA recommends that science teachers adhere to specific safety-related behaviors when performing dissection activities. See p. 137 and *www.nsta.org/about/positions/animals.aspx* for the full text. Here are some expanded comments on the statement:

- Use prepared specimens purchased from a reputable and reliable scientific supply company. An acceptable alternative source for fresh specimens, such as squid or chicken wings, would be a facility—such as a butcher shop, fish market, or supermarket—inspected by the Food and Drug Administration. Using salvaged specimens does not reflect safe practice. This statement is absolutely critical. Salvaged specimens, or "roadkills," can harbor harmful bacteria and other pathogens. Credible fresh specimens eliminate exposure to hazardous chemicals found in preservatives.

- Conduct laboratory and dissection activities in a clean and organized workspace with care and laboratory precision. Good housekeeping is necessary for safety. With fresh specimens, a dirty work space can become a breeding ground for pathogens.

- Conduct dissections in an appropriate physical environment with the proper ventilation, lighting, furniture, and equipment, including hot water and soap for cleanup. Washing hands is a standard operating procedure at all times whenever a laboratory activity is completed. Without proper ventilation, lab occupants would be exposed to potential hazardous vapors from preservatives in specimens.

- Use personal protective equipment (PPE), such as gloves, chemical-splash goggles, and aprons, all of which should be available and used by students, teachers, and visitors to the classroom. PPE is necessary and required when working with materials, such as preservatives and body fluids, that can put eyes in harm's way. Such an activity requires chemical-splash goggles, not just safety glasses.

- Address issues such as allergies and squeamishness about dealing with animal specimens. Given the high frequency of student chemical sensitivities, you must check with students and the school nurse on potential allergies and their symptoms of exposure.

- Ensure that the specimens are handled and disposed of properly. Local or state health departments may be of assistance in this case. Minimally, any preservative should be drained and disposed of according to the directions on the material safety data sheet (MSDS). Dry specimens can then be placed in plastic trash bags and disposed of as refuse, if local sanitation policies allow.

- Ensure that sharp instruments, such as scissors, scalpels, and other tools, are used safely and appropriately. Remind students about sharps and their danger. Have a first-aid action plan should a student receive a cut.

Additional Thoughts

Specific student safety rules for dissection are critical to a successful activity of this type. The Regents Exam Prep Center has a very practical list of safety procedures for students on their internet site (see Resources). The rules are listed as follows:

- Follow all instructions given by your teacher.

- Inform your teacher of any illness as a result of exposure to chemicals used in specimen preparation.

- Avoid contact with preservative chemicals. Rinse the specimens completely before dissection.

- Know where the eyewash fountain is located in case it is needed.

- Wear chemical-splash safety goggles to prevent the splashing of any chemicals into the eyes.

- Properly mount dissection specimens to dissecting pan. Do not dissect a specimen while holding it.

- Handle scalpels or razor blades (safety-edged) with extreme care.

- Always cut away from your body and away from others.

- Never ingest specimen parts.

- Never remove specimens or specimen parts from the classroom—until the dissection is completed, all parts of the dissection must remain within the dissecting pan.

- Properly dispose of dissected materials.

- Store specimens as directed by your teacher.

- Clean up the work area and return all equipment to the proper place when the dissection is completed.

- Wash hands with soap and water after each dissection.

Preservatives

Preservatives for dissection specimens tend to be toxic and hazardous. In most cases, commercial supply houses use formaldehyde, formalin, alcohol, ethylene glycol (Carosafe), or frozen water types of preservatives. Before purchasing any specimens for dissection, obtain the MSDS from the supplier for review and purchase decisions. These are often available online at the supplier's website.

- Formaldehyde, or methanal, is a known nasal and dermal carcinogen. It is also a sensitizer, causing allergy-related symptoms. The bottom line is that no specimens that are preserved in formaldehyde should be used in middle school science.

- Formalin is really an aqueous fluid containing formaldehyde. When the specimens are dissected, formaldehyde can be released. Again, no specimens that are preserved in formalin should be used in middle school sciences.

- Alcohol (usually isopropanol) is very flammable and should also be avoided for preserved dissection specimens if at all possible.

- Ethylene glycol–preserved specimens have actually been first fixed in formaldehyde or formalin solutions. They are then washed and preserved in ethylene glycol. Of the three, ethylene glycol products best minimize student and teacher exposure to formaldehyde. But again, chemical-splash goggles, aprons, and gloves need to be worn if dissection is being done.

Make sure specimens are stored in tightly sealed containers to prevent vaporization of the preservative. Also, label containers with specific preservative information. For example, anything containing alcohol-based preservatives should be labeled "flammable" and "poison."

Alternatives

Alternatives include frozen and freeze-dried specimens. Some specimens, such as fish, squid, and mammal organs, can be found in local supermarkets in the frozen-food section. These should be used in one sitting, because, once they thaw out, they are subject to bacteria growth and should not be reused. Freeze-dried specimens are rehydrated with a dilute alcohol solution and must be rinsed before use.

If science teachers are uncomfortable with doing animal or plant dissections, alternatives include working models, computer software dissection programs, videos, and internet-based dissection programs. Although each of these alternatives sacrifices the formal hands-on experience, there are no hazardous chemical exposure, storage, or disposal issues to deal with or ethical arguments to consider.

The final choice might be fresh specimens secured from a local grocery store or meat market. Without preservatives, these should be refrigerated and used within 24 hours. Because of the potential for bacterial growth, remember to make sure students wash with soap and water after handling the specimens.

Hands-on dissection can be an educationally credible and highly motivating activity when done with respect and safely orchestrated. Quality dissection tools, appropriate ventilation, MSDSs, disposal, storage, and standard operating dissection procedures are all elements that need to be addressed. In addition, appropriate safety guidelines must be in place and enforced.

Internet Resources

NSTA Position Statement: Responsible Use of Live Animals and Dissection in the Science Classroom—*www.www.nsta.org/about/positions/animals.aspx*

Regents Prep: Laboratory Dissection—*http://regentsprep.org/regents/biology/units/laboratory/dissection.cfm*

37. Planting Plants

Why use plants in your science laboratory? First of all, they are an excellent way to implement hands-on, inquiry-based science at the middle school level. Second, plants help students better understand the role of plants in the ecosystem and general environment. Third, plants raise student awareness about specific safety issues related to living organisms used in the laboratory.

Safety Basics

When growing plants in the science laboratory or classroom, you must consider a number of things for safety's sake. For example: What kind of container? What kind of plant? What kind of soil? What kind of pest control? To ensure a meaningful and safe study of plants, consider the following:

- Choose your container based on the potential growth of your plant. The container must provide ample room for root growth and support of the plant. If a small container is selected, you may have to transplant the seedling when it gets too large for its container. Make sure there are drainage holes for excess water to escape. Water, heavy roots, and soil in a container will lead to root rot and bacteria and mold growth. Examples of appropriate containers include plastic or clay commercial pots, cleaned yogurt containers, and egg containers.

- The growing medium must provide good drainage and possibly fertilizer. Commercial potting soil is always an option. One word of caution: Some potting soils containing vermiculite also contain low levels of asbestos. Try alternatives to vermiculite, such as peat moss, bark, or perlite. You can make your own potting soil by mixing equal parts of peat, sand, and soil.

- Yellow leaves are an indication of insufficient fertilizer and/or overwatering. Normal classroom seeds, such as grass or beans, benefit from liquid fertilizers. Liquid fertilizers, however, can burn germinating seeds because they are absorbed faster than solid types. Follow directions as noted on the product. Remember, fertilizers can be considered hazardous materials. Consult the material safety data sheet (MSDS) and follow its precautions.

- Watering plants is critical to their survival, especially in the winter when heating systems cause humidity to plummet in the classroom. Keep the plant soil moist but do not overwater. Soggy soil or pools of water can lead to mold and/or bacteria growth. Desert plants and other succulents are a special case. They should only be watered sparingly, keeping the soil dry.

- Most plants like direct sunlight near a window. Again, know the needs of your plants. If windows for sun-loving plants are not available, commercial light sources can serve as a successful alternative. Remember to make sure the artificial lights are plugged into a wall receptacle that is protected against shock by a ground-fault interrupter (GFI). Contact your facilities director or head custodian if you are unsure about the circuit being GFI protected.

- Moist soil and plants can attract insect pests such as white aphids and white flies. The typical response is to spray pesticides on the plants. This is not a good idea and should not be done. Many pesticides have proven to be a health threat to humans and animals. In fact, many states have pesticide prohibitions that now apply to schools. Alternatives to pesticides include cleaning leaves with soapy water, using alcohol wipes, or just showering the plant with tap water. Physical barriers that attract insects, such as a yellow sticky tape, placed near the base of the plant also can help. Because commercial seeds are often treated with toxic fungicides, students should avoid skin contact with seeds and never place seeds or any plant parts in their mouths. Students should wash their hands after handling plants in the laboratory.

- Some plants, particularly flowering types that release pollen, can be an allergen source for students and teachers. Always check with the school nurse to make sure there are no allergy problems among your students. As noted before, wet pots or soil can also exacerbate mold and fungi allergies. Be attentive to make sure mold or fungi is not growing on plants, soil, or pots.

- Know the identity of every plant used in the classroom. Use only plants that

aren't hazardous to children. Never take specimens from the wild that might include poisonous plants, such as poison ivy, poison oak, or poison sumac. Typical household or holiday plants, such as poinsettias and dieffenbachia, can also be toxic if eaten and should be avoided.

Growing plants in the classroom is very much a part of real science. As in any real science activity, however, safety must be addressed. Teaching students safety through plant study only builds their skills and interest in science.

Resource

Kwan, T., and J. Texley. 2004. *Inquiring safely: A guide for middle school teachers*. Arlington, VA: NSTA Press.

38. Plants to Avoid

When spring is in the air, many science teachers take advantage of the good weather by conducting outdoor labs and taking field trips. Before venturing into the great outdoors with your class, review these plant safety tips.

Poison ivy, poison oak, and poison sumac are the big three that all science teachers know spell *danger*. Many students and teachers are highly allergic to one or more of these plant species. However, this is only the tip of the iceberg. There are more than 500 additional species of plants that can cause everything from an annoying rash to life-threatening allergic reactions.

Safety Precautions for Studying Plants

Any part of a plant—root, stem, leaf, flower, fruit, sap, or juice—has the potential to be poisonous or toxic. In the case of the ivies, the plants secrete oils that cause rashes and itching. If left unchecked, systemic blood infections can result. In addition, dangerous pesticides and herbicides may have been used on the plants. Use the following plant study protocol for safer observation of plant specimens:

- Do not pick plants that are unknown.

- Do not expose the skin or open wounds to any sap or fruit juice.

- Do not eat berries, fruits, roots, seeds, or other plant parts.

- Do not expose eyes or skin, or inhale the smoke of any burning plant parts.

- Place plant specimens collected in plastic bags for observation, but do not touch directly.

- Always wash hands with soap or detergent and water after handling plants.

Signs of Plant Poisoning

Symptoms of plant poisoning can be immediate or long-term. The symptoms are dictated by the mode of delivery, body part exposed and protocol used. The symptoms also vary, depending on the plant and the poison. Symptoms that can be signs of plant poisoning are

- gastrointestinal disturbance,

- increased nasal and salivary secretions,

- rash or itching,

- pupil constriction,

- muscle tremor,

- tightness in the chest,

- convulsions,

- vomiting,

- diarrhea, and

- blueness around the lips and under the fingernails.

Should any of these symptoms be present, immediately contact the school medical support person and/or the poison control center.

Poisonous Plants

Both indoor and outdoor garden plants can cause problems. For example, the foliage of the bird-of-paradise and philodendron plants is toxic. A poinsettia leaf can kill a young child. Outdoor plants such as castor beans are highly dangerous. All parts of the potato and tomato plant are poisonous, except the potato and tomato themselves. Large amounts of rhubarb's leaf blade can be fatal, causing convulsions, coma, and death. These statements are surprising to many people. Science teachers must be knowledgeable about the plants they plan on using in the classroom. Most often, alternatives can and should be used for investigations by students in the science laboratory.

The following list includes some of the more popular and accessible plants that are in some ways poisonous:

- apple (seeds)
- azaleas (all parts)
- bloodroot (all parts)
- buttercup (all parts)
- castor beans
- crocus (all parts)
- delphinium (leaves and seeds)
- dieffenbachia (all parts)
- foxglove (leaves)
- holly (berries of female plant)
- iris (bulb, leaves, and flower stalk)
- jack-in-the-pulpit (all parts)
- lily of the valley (leaves and flowers)
- mistletoe (berries)
- oleander (all parts)
- poinsettia (leaves, stems, and flowers)
- poison hemlock (leaves, stems, and fruit)
- poison ivy (all parts)
- poison oak (all parts)
- privet (leaves and berries)
- rhododendron (leaves)
- rhubarb (leaf blade)
- skunk cabbage (all parts)
- wild black cherry (leaves and pits)
- wild radish (seeds)
- wisteria (pods and seeds)
- yellow jessamine (all parts)
- yew (all parts)

Internet Resources

Many Internet resources provide information on poisonous plants. The following are excellent educational references for teachers:

Cornell University—*www.ansci.cornell. edu/plants/alphalist.html*

University of Pennsylvania—*cal.nbc. upenn.edu/poison*

Botanical.com—*www.botanical.com/ botanical/mgmh/poison.html*

Poisonous Plants and Animals—*library. thinkquest.org/C007974/intro.htm?tqskip 1=1&tqtime=1204*

Yahoo Directory—*dir.yahoo.com/Science/ Biology/Botany?Plants/Poisonous_Plants*

Colorado State University—*www.vth. colostate.edu/poisonous_plants*

39. Animals in the Classroom

Keeping live animals in the classroom or laboratory makes science come alive for students. Animals are the touchstones to real-life experiences of students, and they tend to stimulate curiosity, motivate students, and foster learning. As noted in the National Science Teachers Association's (NSTA's) position statement, Guidelines for Responsible Use of Animals in the Classroom, "Observation and experimentation with living organisms give students unique perspectives of life processes that are not provided by other modes of instruction. Studying animals in the classroom enables students to develop skills of observation and comparison, a sense of stewardship, and an appreciation for the unity, interrelationships, and complexity of life." The position statement goes on to say, "This study, however, requires appropriate, humane care of the organism. Teachers are expected to be knowledgeable about proper care of organisms under study and the safety of their students." (The full position statement can be found at *www. nsta.org/about/positions/animals.aspx.*) The bottom line is that the use of animals in the classroom or laboratory is highly encouraged, providing appropriate care and safety are addressed.

Animal Safety Guidelines

The following guidelines are recommended practice for working with live animals in the science classroom or laboratory:

- The use of animals in the classroom and laboratory must be based on appropriate education objectives and adhere to school policy.

- Student experiments involving animals should not be conducted if they are likely to cause pain, induce nutritional deficiencies, or expose animals to parasites, hazardous chemicals, radiation, or toxic conditions.

- Student experiments involving animals should be presented in writing in advance, reviewed by the science teacher, and conducted under close supervision by the teacher or other trained professional.

- Local, state, and national laws, policies, and regulations relative to the acquisition, care, disposition and temperament, and protection (threatened or endangered status) of animals should be consulted prior to introducing them to the classroom.

- Animals should be inspected for signs of wounds, discharges from the nose or eyes, and excessive scratching before housing them in the classroom or laboratory.

- Cages and related equipment should be sterilized with bleach or Lysol before and after use.

- Be aware of student and employee allergies relative to animals with hair, fur, or feathers. This information can be obtained from the school nurse or by sending home a questionnaire for students' parents to complete.

- At all times, including weekends, holidays, and other times when school is not open, animal habitats must be supplied with appropriate food and water, kept at an appropriate temperature, provided with suitable light, and cleaned of waste. Students should be given the responsibility of caring for and feeding classroom animals.

- Caution should be taken when students bring animals home over vacations and holidays because of potential negative health effects, such as the animal or student contracting colds, influenza, salmonellosis, tuberculosis, or infectious hepatitis. Obtain parental permission in writing before sending any animals home with a student.

- Train students on safety precautions for handling live animals or specimens. Consult a veterinarian or other animal care professional if you need advice.

- Remind students what constitutes inappropriate behavior, such as tapping on glass and poking animals with fingers or other objects.

- Students and employees who have an animal incident, such as scratches or bites, must report immediately to the school medical personnel.

- Make sure animals are protected from chemical cleaners (such as ammonia and harsh detergents), pesticides, and other chemicals used in the care and maintenance of a classroom or lab.

- Animals should not be released into a nonindigenous environment. They can be kept in the classroom, donated to a local nature center, or, in some cases, given to a responsible student with parental permission. Never procure an animal unless you first have a long-term plan for its care.

- You are ultimately responsible for any animals used for instructional purposes in your classroom.

Choose Carefully

For safety's sake, it is advisable to keep only certain types of animals in the classroom or laboratory. Some animals, especially those that bite, scratch, or are poisonous, pose serious threats to students and teachers. The following animals should not be allowed in the school or science classroom or laboratory:

- wild animals, not specifically raised for classroom use

- spiders that are poisonous, such as black widow or brown recluse spiders

- venomous reptiles and fish

- scorpions

- stinging insects such as bees, hornets, and wasps (except those enclosed in self-contained observation hives)

The following animals can be kept in the science classroom/laboratory, but with caution:

- tarantulas

- animals with fur (allergy potential)

- turtles (salmonellosis infection potential)

- birds (psittacosis infection potential)

- fish (bacterial infection potential)

- snails (parasites and bacterial infection potential)

Resources

Montgomery County Public Schools Care of Animals in the Classroom Regulation— *www.mcps.k12.md.us/departments/policy/pdf/ecjrb/pdf*

National Association of Biology Teachers— *www.nabt.org/sub/position statements/animals.asp*

Institute for Laboratory Animal Research— *http://dels.nas.edu/ilar_n/ilarhome/index.shtml*

Kwan, T., and J. Texley. 2002. *Inquiring Safely: A Guide for Middle School Teachers.* Arlington, Va.: NSTA Press.

SECTION
IV

QUESTIONS FROM TEACHERS

GENERAL QUESTIONS

1. Acute or Chronic Effects?

Material safety data sheets (MSDS) seem to always list "acute" and "chronic" effects. What's the difference?

In a nutshell—time of exposure. *Acute effects* are the result of a short exposure to a hazardous chemical, anywhere from a few minutes to several days. A rash or burn caused by a one-time acid exposure is a typical acute effect.

Chronic effects are the result of extended exposure to a hazardous substance. This exposure can last several months or years. Because low doses of the hazardous substance are often involved, the victim is often unaware of the danger. Poisoning from a metal such as arsenic or mercury is a typical chronic effect.

2. Backpacks in Labs?

Students in our school are allowed to bring backpacks to class. Is this a safe practice in a laboratory situation?

Ideally, backpacks should not be allowed in the science laboratory. Some students carry their lunches and other food and drink items in their backpacks, making backpacks attractive nuisances and a great temptation for middle school students. There is the potential for contamination of food and drink products exposed in the laboratory. In addition, backpacks tend to be a tripping hazard.

For students working in science laboratories in which backpacks are allowed, there should also be well-defined behavioral expectations. They should include

- keeping the backpack closed while in the laboratory to prevent food and drink contamination,

- keeping the backpack under either the desk or table and away from the work area and walkways to prevent tripping hazards, and

- having students use caution when putting on or taking off the backpack to prevent hitting something and causing damage.

3. Clothing on Fire

What should I do if a student's clothing catches on fire?

If a student's clothing catches on fire, try to keep the student calm and still. Rapid movements will fan the flames and cause the fire to become more intense. Depending on the circumstances, follow one of the following procedures:

- Smother the flames! If you can reach a fire blanket quickly, you can smother the fire by covering the student with the blanket. The student must be lying on the floor, not standing up. Standing creates a "chimney effect," causing more damage.

- Drop to the floor and roll! The student can drop and roll across the floor to smother the flames if no blanket is available or one is not readily accessible.

- Remove burning clothing! If clothing is loose and can be quickly torn off, it will prevent the student from getting burned further. This can be done before or instead of dropping and rolling or using a fire blanket.

- Water the flame! Providing there is no water-sensitive chemical being used, apply water from a safety shower or other source. Always consult the MSDS (material safety data sheet) before using chemicals to determine the most effective means of firefighting.

Each of these approaches—blanket, drop and roll, removing clothing, and water use—depends on the intensity of flames, amount of clothing, access to a blanket, ability to drop and roll, and other factors.

Training students in lab safety techniques at the beginning of the year and following up with reviews during the school year is the most prudent and protective practice for preventing and dealing with fire in the lab.

4. Eye Protection

Should I require my students to wear eye protection whenever they do activities in the science laboratory?

In a one-word answer—"Yes!" First, the laboratory is a dangerous place, which must be respected at all times. Improper use of glassware, labware, and other science equipment can cause harm to the eyes and face during lab activities. If hazardous liquids such as acids are being used, chemical-splash goggles are required. If solids such as rocks, powders, glass, or metersticks are being used, impact-rated safety glasses or chemical-splash goggles are required. Remember, all occupants, including the teacher, are required by OSHA (Occupational Safety and Health Administration) regulations and state goggle statutes to wear eye protection whenever there is a risk of injuring the eyes.

5. Eyewash Water Temperature

To save money in our budget, my superintendent has recommended that we shut off the water heaters providing tepid water temperatures (60°–100°F) to our eyewash stations and chemical safety shower. Is this an OK idea?

ANSI Standard # Z358.1 requires tepid water for eyewash stations and chemical safety showers. Current research has shown temperatures below 60°F and above 100°F have are harmful to eye tissue. Because the eye must be drenched with water for a minimum of 15 minutes, the water, which would fall below 60°F within a minute or so, would not be at the right temperature. Saving a little money by shutting down heaters does not compare to the potential legal and financial issues in litigation should an accident occur. Also, a licensed science teacher would have some degree of liability, given that the engineering controls (eyewash station) were not operating as required. A teacher in this case would need to alter the curriculum dramatically so that hazardous chemicals would not be used. For many science courses, that would be a problem in itself.

6. Eating in Labs

Is it OK for students to consume food or drink in a science laboratory?

"Never bring food or drink into the laboratory or work space. Do not eat or drink any substances being tested unless expressly permitted to do so by your teacher."

These two sentences are common statements listed in laboratory safety procedures. Professional guidelines stress that eating food in a laboratory is unacceptable. There are a number of overt and covert means through which students and teachers can find their food or drink contaminated by eating or drinking in a laboratory. The contamination can be a serious burden to one's immediate health, and, in some cases, survival.

There may be isolated instances in which food or drink can be consumed in the laboratory, providing appropriate procedures are in place. For example, if it is necessary for a student to drink water while in the laboratory, bottled water with a sports cap top should be required. In such a case, there should be clear procedures set up and approved by the chemical hygiene officer or science supervisor or building principal for eating or drinking in the laboratory.

7. Protecting Feet

Should I require students to wear closed-toe shoes when doing experiments in eighth-grade physical science?

Yes! Closed-toe shoes should be standard operating procedure in all laboratory work. Accidents happen when glassware falls to the floor and smashes, chemicals get spilled on the floor, or weights fall off workbenches. Everyone should keep feet covered with at least sneakers, or regular shoes that expose no skin. Remind students the day before a laboratory that closed-toe shoes are required for the upcoming lab. Be ready to enforce your policy. If the student is allowed to wear open-toe shoes, such as sandals, and gets hurt, the teacher has liability.

8. Plasticware or Glassware?

Should I use plasticware or glassware in my middle school science laboratory?

In most cases, plasticware would be the safer choice. For example, polypropylene has great chemical resistance, except for use with organic solvents and strong oxidizers. It has a much higher resistance to breaking or shattering. The key word is resistance. Shattering or breaking glass (and, on rare occasion, plastic) is always a concern. Students should wear chemical-splash goggles when working with any laboratory equipment, including plasticware or glassware. Although plasticware such as polymethylpentene can withstand temperatures up to 175°C, plasticware should not be heated or be used in any type of high-temperature exothermic reactions.

9. Housekeeping Regulations

What are some general rules about housekeeping in the middle school science laboratory?

Housekeeping practices are critical to maintaining a safe working environment for both the teacher and students. The Occupational Safety and Health Administration (OSHA) General Housekeeping Standard [CFR 1910.141(a)(3)] and Laboratory Standard [CFR 1910.1450] directly apply to keeping a laboratory safe and orderly. Several items profile good housekeeping, including:

- Store chemicals on shelves in classroom or storeroom cabinets. Never store them on the floor or under the fume hood.

- Avoid slip and fall hazards by making sure spilled liquids are cleaned up immediately after being spilled; glassware, lab ware, and other small items are kept off the floor; and electrical cords are off the floor or covered.

- Keep aisles open and free of obstructions such as desks, chairs, equipment, and refuse containers.

- Clear workbenches of unused materials.

- Close cabinets and drawers while working in the laboratory.

- Store goggles and aprons in appropriate cabinets and drawers.

10. Locking the Lab

Should my science laboratory have a special key?

The Occupational Safety and Health Administration (OSHA) considers science laboratories to be secured areas, similar to electrical closets and boiler rooms. They are dangerous places for which employees need special training for safer operation.

Given that interpretation, school science laboratories should have unique locks and keys with access limited to science teachers, administrators, and trained maintenance and custodial personnel.

11. Overcrowded Labs

How can I work with my principal so he can understand my concern about the safety dangers of an overcrowded science laboratory?

Be aware that the principal may well understand the issue but is getting pressure from elsewhere. The first line of action is education. In many cases, principals are not aware that safety codes even exist for occupancy load in science laboratories. As the science teacher, your job is to help the principal be an advocate for your cause. You might consider putting your concerns in writing and asking for a meeting to discuss the issue. Also remember that there is strength in numbers! Try to get support from science colleagues in the department.

An example of such an introductory letter follows. Understand that codes do vary from state to state and therefore you need to do your homework first.

Sample letter:

Dear Principal _____:

The National Science Education Standards, State Science Frameworks, The National Science Teachers Association, and other professional science organizations encourage and foster hands-on, process- and inquiry-based science instruction. In the same spirit, "No Child Left Behind" federal legislation will be requiring science assessment by states starting in 2007–2008.

To best prepare our students for instruction and assessments, appropriate laboratory facilities are critical for academic and safety reasons. Building and fire codes have established occupancy loads for science laboratories, similar to auditoriums, gymnasiums, cafeterias, and so on, to ensure safety and orderly egress in case of an emergency.

We are concerned about the current numbers of students in our school's occupied laboratory spaces relative to safety codes. We would like the opportunity to share our concerns with you as the chief building administrator and explore viable alternative solutions. We look forward to working with you on this concern in the near future.

Sincerely,

---

12. Microwave Ovens

Are microwave ovens safe to use for heating liquids for experiments?

Microwaves can be a safer alternative to gas burners and hot plates but do have limitations. Review the following general tips, which can be helpful for safer operation:

- Limit the use of microwaves to heating water or other "safe" liquids. Do not put flammable liquids, such as alcohol, in the microwave.

- Check the electrical cord for cuts, frayed wires, or wire exposure.

- Use an inexpensive microwave detector to check for leaks.

- Remove lids or caps from containers. Never cook eggs in the shell. Also, prick the yolk before cooking.

- Never turn on an empty microwave.

- Make sure the microwave is clean and in good operating condition. Using dish detergent and water, clean the inside, the door, and the seal.

- Never operate the oven when something is caught in the door.

- Make sure "Caution: Microwave in Use" sign is posted.

- Make sure no metal parts, such as metal twist ties from bags, are placed in the oven.

13. Old Counters and Tabletops

"I have 30- to 40-year-old, black-topped lab tables and counters in my room. They do not have a shiny look on their surface. Despite constant cleaning, the students still complain that the counters and tables are dirty. This has been the case for the five years I have been in this room. Each time I wipe the lab tables with plain water or with water and cleaning materials, black color rubs off of them onto the sponge or cloth. On examination, no solid bits or pieces can be seen in the black color. What are these tables and counters made of? What is this black color? Is it possibly asbestos? Is it some other dangerous material? What can we do to fix this problem? What would be the cost?"

Your question is a good one! Those tables can, indeed, harbor chemicals, bacteria, or other harmful things in those cracks. That's why it's standard practice never to eat in a science laboratory and to clean surfaces regularly with a disinfectant.

Now, what are those tables made of? Jim Biehle of Inside/Out Architecture in Clayton, Missouri, offers this advice: "If the surface is still sound (except for digs made by sharp objects) they may be epoxy resin. If the surface is pitted, it's likely that they're particle board with a melamine coating. The melamine may have been penetrated, and the moisture caused the core particle board to expand. Sanding would get rid of the surface pockmarks, but, if the underlying particle board is bad, they would come back as soon as they get wet again, and the tables wouldn't be worth recoating. If the tables are only 30 years old, they probably don't have any asbestos in them or lead-based paint, as both of these materials were banned by this time." However, if your tables are older or if you are unsure of their age, don't touch them or try to resurface them. If your tables have turned a lighter gray in color and are rock-hard like epoxy, this may be an indication that they contain asbestos. Ask your district asbestos-certified supervisor to check out any questionable tables.

Old epoxy resin tables can be refinished with a product available from science furnishings vendors. Chris Lambert of Sheldon Laboratory Equipment explains: "Our supplier offers a finishing kit that contains materials to repair surface scratches and also finishing oil to apply to tops after they been cleaned to help restore their luster." You can have the tables refinished with good results, but the process is hazardous. Teachers should contact school custodial or maintainer supervisors to request refinishing by qualified school personnel or an outside contractor.

14. Goggle Sanitizers

How do you operate a goggle sanitizer correctly?

Goggle sanitizers are ultraviolet sterilization cabinets used to reduce the risks of transferring specific eye and skin infections between students who are sharing chemical-splash goggles. The sterilization procedure allows students in more than one class to safely share their personal protective eyewear.

Instructions on sanitizers call for the goggles to be loaded on a racking system in the cabinet. Note: Goggles should not be stacked on top of one another because this will compromise the sterilization process. The cabinet door is then locked and a timer is engaged, which floods the inside of the cabinet with ultraviolet (UV) light for approximately 15 minutes. The UV light is germicidal in nature and serves to reduce the number of pathogenic microorganisms. Unfortunately, the UV light has poor penetrating power, and dust, dirt, and other barriers on the bulb can prevent the light from reaching microorganisms on the goggles. To ensure maximum penetration, the bulb should be cleaned monthly or more (depending on use or visual inspection) by unplugging the sanitizer and wiping the bulb with an alcohol-moistened cloth. Sanitizers have a peekhole through which the user can check to make sure the bulb is glowing purple. If the purple glow is missing, change the bulb.

15. Cleaning With Sponges

Should sponges be used for lab station cleanup and wipeup? If so, how often should they be replaced?

Sponges are often used for lab station cleanup because they absorb spills and, unlike paper towels, can be reused. However, the convenience comes with a price! Bacteria can grow on a sponge because of the nutrients and moisture it provides to support growth. By using the same dirty sponge over a short period of time, bacteria can be transferred (in a matter of minutes) from one surface to another, including the user's hand.

Look for pure cellulose sponges without disinfectants. A statement such as "contains antimold growth agent" on the sponge's wrapper usually indicates the presence of a disinfectant. Most sponges contain a synthetic disinfectant such as triclosan. The Environmental Protection Agency (EPA) registers triclosan as a pesticide. The chemical can be spread wherever the sponge is used.

To minimize health and safety issues, sponges should be decontaminated regularly. There are several means available to the middle school science teacher to decontaminate sponges:

- Heat the contaminated WET sponge for one minute in a microwave on the high setting. There could be a slight odor depending on the sponge, but nothing major.

- Soak contaminated sponges for about five minutes in a solution of bleach (10 percent minimum). A prepared solution of bleach can be purchased and used. Keep all bleach away from ammonia because the two chemicals will react and produce a poisonous gas.

- Place the sponge in a dishwasher along with glassware and run it through the wash cycle, using detergent and hot water.

If decontamination is done regularly, sponges will be less of a health and safety risk and more of a housekeeping tool for cleanup. Once sponges start deteriorating (falling apart), it is time to purchase new ones.

16. Safer Shelving

I have had chemicals fall off the shelves in my chemical storeroom. How can I prevent this from happening?

Lip-edged wooden shelving anchored into the wall is an effective means of preventing chemicals from falling off the shelves. The lip-edge is a raised barrier about 2.5 cm above the front of the shelves that prevents most chemical containers from rolling off. Simple floor or wall vibrations can put these containers in motion. Should the container of a hazardous chemical fall to the floor and crack open, it could present a very dangerous situation. Wooden shelves are recommended for chemical storage because they are relatively inert to chemical reactions such as rusting or corroding from vapors.

17. Substitutes and Hands-On Labs

Can I have a substitute do hands-on laboratory work with my students if I am absent from work?

Only if a certified science teacher is available to act as a substitute should you consider assigning hands-on laboratory work when you aren't present. Only seatwork should be assigned if a noncertified substitute will be in charge of the class.

18. Synthetic Nails

Should I be concerned about female students with long synthetic fingernails when they are working with flames?

If you have ever entered a nail salon, you will know that you can sense right away the flammable vapors in the air. Synthetic fingernails are made of extremely flammable polymers. They have the potential to catch on fire when someone is using a Bunsen burner or candle. Once this happens, the nails tend to burn completely because their material makes a fire very difficult to extinguish. Work with your administration, and develop written policies on appropriate laboratory attire that include a warning about the danger of synthetic nails in the lab. Share the policies with parents at the beginning of the school year. If a student with synthetic nails does show up for a lab involving flames, provide an alternative such as a hot plate, if possible, or ask the student to serve as a recorder or assume another role that doesn't require her to be close to flames.

19. Water Bottles

Should I allow students to drink in the science lab?

Drinking in school science labs depends on school rules and practices. The Occupational Safety and Health Administration (OSHA) housekeeping rules and Hazard Communication Standard rule discourage food and drink in the laboratory. Prudent practice certainly enforces the same behaviors. Realistically, although no food or eating should be allowed, students might be allowed to use water bottles with secured sports caps. Regular screw-cap bottles should not be permitted.

20. Holding Chemicals for Absentees

How long should chemicals—solutions, lab setups, for example—be held for students who are absent?

The answer to this question depends on several factors. First, some solutions have expiration dates. For example, a solution containing Vitamin C can be rendered useless after a few hours. Seek references to determine the "life" of the chemicals you are using. Second, make sure there is adequate and appropriate storage space for these items. Depending on the type of chemicals, locked cabinets in the lab, the chemical storeroom, or other appropriate secured locations may be used. Third, you should have a policy on make-up deadlines for laboratories missed in place for students. One final thought: If the disposal of these solutions requires a commercial hazardous-waste or items-to-be-recycled contractor, make sure the activity is completed by the pick-up timeline.

21. Alcohol Burner Dangers

Should I use alcohol burners as a heat source for my seventh-grade science class?

Before answering that question, I'd like to share with you the following safety incident:

"Students in a high school science lab were allowed to fill empty alcohol burners using a funnel and a container of alcohol located on a side bench. When the funnel was misplaced, students began filling the burners directly from the container. Alcohol was spilled on the lab bench. When a student approached the bench with a still-glowing burner, a fire ensued in which the alcohol container was knocked over and a student was drenched in alcohol. The student was eventually knocked to the floor and the flames extinguished. Unfortunately it was too late and the student died of her burns" (Anecdotal Accidents, Chemical Health and Safety, September/October 1995).

Although alcohol burners are convenient to use, they are extremely dangerous as this reference points out. There are numerous other reports of similar accidents in the press and on the internet. Fortunately, most do not include a fatality. Sadly, most do include scarred victims. Many school districts have banned the use of alcohol burners as heat sources and suggest using hot plates instead. Bunsen burners should be used only on a limited basis, because they can be dangerous unless there was effective training and supervision. Alcohol burners are unpredictable and use a highly flammable fuel. Bottom line: For safety's sake, get rid of the alcohol burners!

22. Chemical Hazards Guide

Is there a free or relatively inexpensive resource that can address chemical hazards in the science laboratory?

NIOSH (National Institute for Occupational Safety and Health) has an exceptional resource guide titled NIOSH Pocket Guide to Chemical Hazards. It provides general industrial hygiene information on several hundred chemicals. Information about getting this guide online, printed or in CD format, is available at *www.cdc.gov/niosh/npg/npg.html.*

23. Chemical Disposal

I have inherited a very old chemistry closet with chemicals that are missing labels and are eating through bottles—what a mess! There are no MSDSs [material

safety data sheets], and I need to know where to get them. We had a number of very dangerous problems this past school year. I am having all unlabeled or deteriorating bottles removed by a licensed company. Any advice?

Any chemicals missing labels or in compromised containers must be professionally removed and appropriately disposed of by a licensed and bonded chemical disposal company. Make sure it is reputable by checking with your state's Better Business Bureau for the company's history on complaints and credibility.

For the MSDS sheets, if there is a label, try contacting the chemical company noted and ask for the specific MSDS. If that is not available, there are a number of free and subscription websites having MSDS. Two useful sites are:

MSDS Search at *www.msdssearch.com*. This is a national repository.

MSDS on the internet at *www.ilpi. com/msds*. This excellent site lists specific free and subscription MSDS websites on the internet.

24. Chemical Hygiene Officers

What is a chemical hygiene officer and do we need one at a middle school?

A chemical hygiene officer, or CHO, is a person designated by the employer (board of education) who provides technical guidance in the development and implementation of the chemical hygiene plan. The position and plan are required for schools that are under the jurisdiction of either the federal OSHA (Occupational Safety and Health Administration) or a state equivalent. This covers most states and schools in the country. The CHO usually is a chemistry teacher, science supervisor or chairperson, technician, or science paraprofessional. The bottom line is that the CHO must be knowledgeable

in working with chemicals to provide technical guidance.

25. Cleaning Safety Goggles

What is an effective way to clean safety goggles?

Safety goggle hygiene is important for several reasons. Goggles can transfer the bacteria and viruses responsible for pinkeye and other illnesses. Dirty goggles can also distort the field of vision, which can cause you to mishandle equipment and hazardous chemicals. Dirt can also mask cracks that compromise the protective barrier the goggles should provide.

There are several means for cleaning goggles. The most common and most expensive is using a goggle sanitizer. This device usually utilizes ultraviolet technology to destroy bacteria and sanitize the goggles. Bathing goggles in solutions containing detergent (1 part detergent to 25 parts water) and other cleaning agents is another option. Goggles can be air or towel dried, depending on when they will be needed again. Alcohol wipes can also be used, but they can damage some types of goggles. Check with your goggle manufacturer before using alcohol wipes.

Some schools believe that the hygiene problem is avoided if they have students purchase their own goggles. Actually, this may cause even more problems because students may not clean them as often or thoroughly as they should. The school should be responsible for making sure the goggles—no matter who owns them—are clean, sanitized, and the proper type for the activity in question.

The school's chemical hygiene plan should have a written policy on the proper cleaning of safety goggles. It should be shared with students at the beginning of every science course in which goggles are to be used.

26. Copper Sulfate Substitute

In my daughter's sixth-grade middle school class, the teacher had students grind copper sulfate crystals using a mortar and pestle to observe the dissolution of the powdered crystals in water. When my daughter balked at handling the stuff (she had read the warnings on the label), the teacher tried to calm her fears by letting her stir her fingers through the crystals to show that they were safe. Having heard this from my daughter, I shared my concern with the teacher about this incident. In response, the teacher indicated that she would welcome any safe alternatives for use in this lab that I could give her. What can I suggest to her as a safe alternative?

First, let me state that as chemicals go, copper sulfate is a skin and respiratory irritant, in addition to being moderately toxic by ingestion and inhalation. This is one of those chemicals that really should be removed from middle school science labs—especially in this case, given the fact that students were grinding the chemical into fine powder, which could become airborne and inhaled.

If the purpose of the lesson is simply to see the distribution of the solute in the solvent, concentrated drink products such as Crystal Light, available at most supermarkets, come in a spectrum of colors and are a much safer alternative to copper sulfate. Freeze-dried tea, which comes in different colors, is another alternative that comes to mind. Both of these products exhibit the same end result as the use of copper sulfate with one major exception—they are safe to use! Bottom line is science should be both fun and safe. And the use of common items by students provides touchstones to real life—thus fostering science literacy.

27. MSDS—Easy Access

Do I need to keep material safety data sheets [MSDSs] handy?

Material safety data sheets, or MSDSs, provide teachers and students with critical information about the hazards of chemicals they are using. The Occupational Safety and Health Administration (OSHA) requires MSDSs to be readily available or accessible for employee use. It is recommended that science teachers keep MSDSs for those chemicals in use during a specific class period in a folder near the door to the laboratory. Should there be an incident or accident, students, teachers, administrators, and school medical support personnel will know where they can immediately access this information. Remember, teachers can also have accidents with hazardous chemicals. Quick access to this vital information can save your life!

28. MSDS Information

Why don't all material safety data sheets [MSDSs] look the same?

The Occupational Safety and Health Administration (OSHA) prescribes the minimum type of information that is required on MSDS, but not the order or format in which the information is presented. On the MSDS, manufacturers and suppliers of hazardous chemicals are required to provide the user with the following information: the name of the chemical; physical/chemical characteristics; physical hazards; health hazards; exposure levels; known or suspected carcinogenic properties; control measures; first-aid procedures; date of MSDS preparation; name, address, and phone number of party responsible for preparing or revising the MSDS; and emergency phone numbers in case of an accident.

29. Transporting Chemicals

My storage and preparation rooms are down the corridor from my science laboratory. How can I safely transport chemicals and labware from one location to the other?

First of all, the more congested or crowded the hall, the more unsafe it is to transport materials. Transport materials only while students are in class, or before or after school when few occupants are in the corridor. Never transport materials between class periods.

Containers should be put in protective carrying devices. Remember that glassware breaks very easily if dropped or bumped. Carry only what can be held in your hands. Do not hold containers close to your body when in transit. If you bump into something or someone, the container could drop and smash, or break against your body. This could create direct contact with sharp objects and hazardous chemicals.

In situations where you have much to carry, use a sturdy cart with rims or lips on each shelf. Never transport incompatible chemicals at the same time. Also, wear full personal protective devices such as gloves, chemical-splash goggles, and an apron.

30. Bunsen Burner Tubing

Can I use thin, amber-colored, latex tubing to connect Bunsen burners to the gas source?

If you need to use Bunsen burners in the science laboratory as a heat source at the middle school level, any tubing selected should meet the American Gas Association (AGA) standards. It is usually a galvanized flexible metal tube with gas-tight connectors.

The problem with thin, amber latex rubber tubing is that over time it dries out, cracks, and provides the opportunity for a gas leak and explosion. It also does not necessarily provide for a gas-tight connection. It should not be used. The thicker, black rubber tubing can be used as an acceptable alternative.

31. Safer Gas Valves

Our lab was redone last summer, without any input from the science teachers, and our gas valves now are outfitted with four-point knobs. It is hard to describe them, but they are the same as our water faucet controls in shape. The difficulty is that they need to be turned at least one full rotation, possibly two or three, in order for the gas to flow through the jet. Should I ask for the four-point knobs to be replaced?

Acceptable and prudent practice dictates that gas fixtures in the laboratory have a single control lever, a pedestal base, and a serrated hose connection. The type of control knob you describe is a safety problem in that it is not possible to determine if the valve is open or closed by visual inspection. From a safety standpoint, I certainly would suggest a retrofit with conventional gas valves.

Teachers need to be involved in the planning of new or renovated science facilities. As professionals, you are aware of issues that need to be addressed and might be overlooked by contractors.

32. Ether Substitutes

Can ether be safely used to anesthetize fruit flies in a lab?

No! Besides being extremely flammable, ether easily forms peroxides that are explosive. Ether should never be used in a middle school science laboratory. There are commercially available anesthetic supplies from biological supply companies that can safely be used, such as FlyNap or Carbon Dioxide Anesthetizer. Always remember to have adequate laboratory ventilation that will accommodate use of anesthetizers.

33. Classroom Critters

I am thinking of having newts and salamanders in the classroom and am wondering about safety.

Animals can be a wonderful and exciting addition to the middle school science laboratory or science classroom. Their presence can lead to many teachable moments for students and can prove highly motivating. However, several issues need to be addressed before their arrival:

- Approval from administration: First, notify and secure approval from the principal, science supervisor, or similar school official. They may be aware of policies, regulations, or accepted practices for having animals in the classroom or laboratory. Boards of education often have policy statements on using live animals in the science classroom or laboratory. If there is no policy, science teachers should consider taking a leadership role in helping the administration develop such a policy.

- Source of animals: Vertebrate animals should not be removed from their environment by teachers or students for use in the classroom. Animals should be secured only from reputable commercial

biological supply houses. You also may be able to borrow specimens from local museums, nature centers, and animal care groups.

- Care of the animals: Animals in captivity have special needs that must be addressed—food, water, shelter, and housekeeping, to name a few. Students can accept responsibility in some of these areas. Those assigned to cleaning cages should always wear gloves and wash their hands thoroughly afterward.

- Health hazards for students and teacher: Animals can present health hazards for some students and their teacher. Allergies are usually the biggest problem. Science teachers need to let parents know about animals coming into the classroom or laboratory and if allergies are a problem for students.

- Handling of animals: The possibility of such hazards as disease transfer from bites and skin injuries need to be addressed by rules established for student interaction with animals. Consider using special protective covering on hands such as leather or latex gloves when having students handle animals after appropriate training. The National Science Teachers Association (NSTA) position statement, "Responsible Use of Live Animals and Dissection in the Science Classroom," is available at *www.nsta.org/about/positions/animals.aspx* and on page 133.

- Sensitivity to animals: Take to prevent accidents to and suffering by the animals. Be attentive to surroundings like temperature, humidity, and other survival requirements.

- Animal rights groups: In the event of a visit from an animal rights group demanding to know why you keep animals in the classroom, be prepared to defend your decision. When asked why I choose to keep animals in the classroom, I respond that it teaches students about the needs of animals, their habitats, how to care for them, and most importantly, to respect them.

34. Microscope Use

Are there any health or safety issues associated with students using microscopes?

Oculars, or eyepiece lenses, can potentially be sites for the communicable disease-causing bacteria and viruses that lead to pinkeye or conjunctivitis. To prevent the transfer of microbes, the contact area on the lens should be cleaned with isopropyl alcohol each time a different student uses it.

Another safety problem can occur if students use direct sunlight as a light source for the microscope. The condensed sunlight can cause eye damage.

A final safety concern is with microscope electrical cords. Before each use, students should inspect the cords for frayed or broken wires and plugs. Also caution students not to touch the metal clips on the plugs when inserting them into an electrical wall receptacle. Students can get shocked in these cases, even when using a ground-fault-circuit-interrupter (GFCI) protected circuit. Keep water away from the scope work area except for very small quantities transferred by pipette to prepare slides.

35. Communication on Field Trips

Field experiences are a critical part of our middle school science curriculum. Any suggestions for keeping the lines of communication open when in the field?

Many schools today are solving this problem by embracing technology. If you take your class into the field, bring along a walkie-talkie or cell phone in case you have an emergency. Visit the site before-hand to make sure that your cell phone is operational and your walkie-talkie is within range of the other unit. Also, check the batteries in your device before heading out into the field. If your school hasn't already done so, ask them to invest in a cell phone or set of walkie-talkies that would be available to teachers working with their students in the field.

36. Petri Plate Disposal

I use petri plates to grow mold and bacteria in my seventh-grade life science lab. What is a safe way to dispose of them?

First, extreme caution should be exercised when mold or bacteria are being cultured on petri plates in the middle school science laboratory. Make sure they are completely sealed after being inoculated or exposed to bacteria and mold spores or cultures. Prepared slides are an excellent alternative to observing specimens and should be considered in lieu of using living bacteria and mold specimens.

Autoclaving is the safest method for sterilizing used petri dishes. They can be autoclaved at 121° C at 15 psi for 30 minutes before discarding. Following autoclaving, place them in a plastic bag, close the bag, and put it into a dumpster. Never leave them in laboratory or office wastebaskets where they can pose a hazard to janitorial staff. If you don't have an autoclave, your district high school may have one in its biology department.

37. Terrariums

What do I need to know about keeping classroom plants in a terrarium?

First of all, a classroom terrarium is a great tool for studying ecosystems. It can be purchased from biological supply houses or created using an aquarium, large jar, or even plastic bag. The soil should contain a mixture of peat moss, potting soil, sand, and activated charcoal to absorb decaying organic material from the soil and water. Also, to keep the humidity within agreeable levels, use a loose-fitting lid for regular plants and no lid for cacti or other succulents. If animals are used, be sure there are no means of escape from the terrarium. As with regular potted plants, watch for signs of overwatering, such as mold growth, or underwatering, such as yellow leaves.

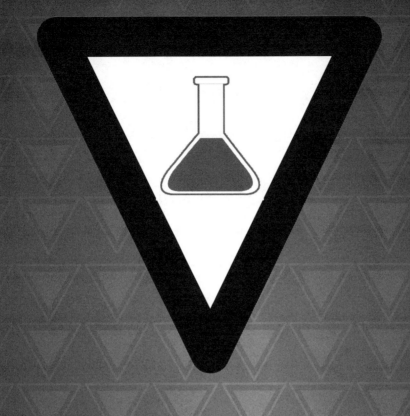

APPENDICES

◁ NSTA POSITION STATEMENTS

Safety and School Science Instruction

Preamble

Inherent in many instructional settings including science is the potential for injury and possible litigation. These issues can be avoided or reduced by the proper application of a safety plan.

Rationale

High quality science instruction includes laboratory investigations, interactive or demonstration activities, and field trips.

Declarations

The National Science Teachers Association recommends that school districts and teachers adhere to the following guidelines:

- School districts must adopt written safety standards, hazardous material management and disposal procedures for chemical and biological wastes. These procedures must meet or exceed the standards adopted by EPA, OSHA and/or appropriate state and local agencies.

- School authorities and teachers share the responsibility of establishing and maintaining safety standards.

- School authorities are responsible for providing safety equipment (i.e., fire extinguishers), personal protective equipment (i.e., eyewash stations, goggles), material safety data sheets and training appropriate for each science teaching situation.

- School authorities will inform teachers of the nature and limits of liability and tort insurance held by the school district.

- All science teachers must be involved in an established and ongoing safety training program relative to the established safety procedures which is updated on an annual basis.

- Teachers shall be notified of individual student health concerns.

- The maximum number of occupants in a laboratory teaching space shall be based on the following:
  - the building and fire safety codes;
  - occupancy load limits;
  - design of the laboratory teaching facility;
  - appropriate supervision and the special needs of students.

- Materials intended for human consumption shall not be permitted in any space used for hazardous chemicals and/or materials.

- Students and parents will receive written notice of appropriate safety regulations to be followed in science instructional settings.

References

Section 1008.0 Occupant Load—BOCA National Building Code/1996

Section 10-1.7.0 Occupant Load—NFPA Life Safety Code 101-97

40 CFR 260-70 Resource Conservation and Recovery Act (RCRA)

29 CFR 1910.1200 Hazard Communication Standard (Right to Know Law)

29 CFR 1910.1450 Laboratory Standard, Part Q The Laboratory Standard (Chemical Hygiene Law)

National Research Council (NRC) 1995. *Prudent practices in the laboratory.* Washington, DC: National Academy Press.

Furr, K., ed. 1995. *Handbook of laboratory safety, 4th ed.* Boca Raton, FL: CRC Press.

Fleming, et al., eds. 1995. *Laboratory safety, 2nd ed.* Washington, DC: ASM Press.

National Science Education Leadership Position Paper. 1997. Class size in laboratory rooms. *The Navigator* 33(2).

Authors

George R. Hague, Jr., Chair Science Safety Advisory Board, St. Mark's School of Texas, Dallas, TX 75230

Douglas Mandt, Immediate Past-Chair Science Safety Advisory Board, Science Education Consultant, Edgewood, WA 98372

Dennis D. Bromley, Safety Instructor, Independent Contractor, Anchorage, AK 99502

Donna M. Brown, Radnor Township School District, Wayne, PA 19087

Frances S. Hess, Cooperstown H.S., Cooperstown, NY 13326

Lorraine Jones, Kirby H.S., Nashville, TN

William F. McComas, Director NSTA District XVI, University of Southern California, Los Angeles, CA 90089

Kenneth Roy, Glastonbury Public Schools, Glastonbury, CT 06033

Linda D. Sinclair, South Carolina Department of Education, Columbia, SC 29201

Colette Skinner, Henderson, NV 89015

Olivia C. Swinton, Patricia-Roberts Harris Education Center, Washington, DC

Nina Visconti-Phillips, Assistance & Resources Integrating Science Education (ARISE) Dayton, NJ 08810

—Adopted by the NSTA Board of Directors
July 2000

Liability of Science Educators for Laboratory Safety

Introduction

Laboratory investigations are essential for the effective teaching and learning of science. A school laboratory investigation ("lab") is an experience in the laboratory, classroom, or the field that provides students with opportunities to interact directly with natural phenomena or with data collected by others using tools, materials, data collection techniques, and models (NRC 2006, p. 3). Inherent in laboratory-based activities is the potential for injury. Studies show that safety in K–12 school science instruction needs immediate and significant attention. (Gerlovich et al. 2005)

As professionals, teachers of science have a duty of care to ensure the safety of students, teachers, and staff. Duty of care is defined as an obligation, recognized by law, requiring conformance to a certain standard of conduct to protect others against unreasonable risk (Prosser et al. 1984). "The breach of a particular duty owed to a student or others may lead to liability for both the teacher and the school district that employs that teacher" (Ryan 2001). As such, science educators must act as a reasonably prudent person would in providing and maintaining a safe learning environment for their students.

Educators' duty to maintain a safe learning environment while providing science instruction *also* must be shared by school leaders, district administrators, school boards, parents, and students. It is vital that teachers and administrators communicate regularly and fully on the essentials of safe instruction for students.

Declarations

To ensure a safe and effective learning environment for students, teachers of science should

- Integrate laboratory investigations into science instruction so that all students—including students with academic, remedial, or physical needs; gifted and talented students; and English language learners—have the opportunity to participate in laboratory investigations in a safe environment (NSTA 2007).

- Be proactive in *Seeking* professional development opportunities to learn and implement practices and procedures necessary to conduct safe laboratory science investigations, including storage, use, and disposal of materials and chemicals; use of personal protective equipment; engineering controls; and proper administrative procedures (Roy 2006).

- Request and encourage school and district leadership to provide necessary professional development opportunities for staff and take personal professional responsibility to learn and implement these safe practices and procedures into teaching.

- Exercise reasonable judgment when conducting laboratory investigations.

- Accept the duty of care to provide all students and staff with a safe environment while performing hands-on science investigations or demonstrations in the laboratory, classroom, or field setting; using, storing, disposing/recycling, or transporting chemicals; or engaging in other related activities.

- Modify or alter activities in a safe manner, or select alternative activities to perform, when in the exercise of their duty, they determine that the proposed activities cannot be performed safely or a safe environment cannot be maintained.

- Identify, document, and notify school and district officials about existing or potential safety issues that impact the learning environment, including hazards such as class-size overcrowding in violation of occupancy load codes (BOCA 1996, ICC 2003, NFPA 2006) or contrary to safety research (West et al. 2005), inadequate or defective equipment, inadequate number or size of labs, or improper facility design (Motz et al. 2007), and give necessary recommendations to correct the issue or rectify a particular situation. Overcrowding has two research-based safety concerns: sufficient supervision and adequate individual workspace. Classes containing more than 24 students engaged in science activities cannot safely be supervised by one teacher. Additionally, research data show that accidents rise dramatically as class enrollments exceed 24 students or when inadequate individual workspace is provided (West et al. 2005).

- Communicate fully and regularly (at least once quarterly) with administrators regarding issues impacting the provision of safe science instruction.

- Share the responsibility with school district officials in establishing and implementing written safety standards, policies, and procedures, and ensure their compliance.

- Understand the scope of the duty of care in acting as a reasonably prudent person in providing science instruction, and acknowledge the limitations of insurance in denying coverage for reckless and intentional acts, as well as the potential for individual liability for acts outside the course and scope of employment. [See generally, Restatement (Second) of Torts §202. 1965; Anderson et al. 1999, p. 398.]

- To ensure a safe learning environment, school district officials—such as administrators, principals, assistant principals, science supervisors, and superintendents—should:

- Understand that for science to be taught properly and effectively, lab activities—conducted in the laboratory, classroom, or field setting—must be integrated fully and safely into the science curriculum (NSTA 2007).

- Develop and implement comprehensive safety policies with clear procedures for engaging in lab activities. These safety policies should comply with all applicable local and state health and safety codes, regulations, ordinances, and other rules established by the applicable oversight organization, including the Occupational Safety & Health Administration (OSHA), International Code Council (ICC), Building Officials and Code Administrators (BOCA), and National Fire Protection Association (NFPA).

- Ensure that all safety policies, including those related to safety training, are reviewed and updated annually in consultation with school or district science educators.

- Support and encourage the use of laboratory investigations in science instruction, and share the responsibility with teachers to develop and fully integrate these activities into the science curriculum.

- Become knowledgeable of and enforce all local, state, and federal codes and regulations to ensure a safe learning environment for students and educators. Particular attention should be given to means of hazard prevention, including reasonable class sizes to prevent overcrowding in violation of occupancy load codes (BOCA 1996, ICC 2003, NFPA 2006) or contrary to safety research (West et al. 2005); replacement or repair of inadequate or defective equipment; adequate number or size of labs (Motz et al. 2007), or proper facility design; and the proper use, storage, disposal, or recycling of chemicals.

- Understand that the number of occupants allowed in the laboratory must be set at a safe level based on building and fire safety codes, size and design of the laboratory teaching facility, chemical/physical/biological hazards, and students' needs (NSTA 2000; Roy 2006). Science classes should have no more than 24 students to allow for adequate supervision during science activities, even if the occupancy load limit might accommodate more (NSTA 2004). It is equally important to ensure adequate workspace for each student. NSTA recommends 60 sq. ft. for each secondary student and 45 sq. ft. for each elementary student in a laboratory/classroom setting (Motz et al. 2007). Research data show that accidents rise dramatically as class enrollments exceed 24 students or when inadequate individual workspace is provided (West et al. 2005).

- Require teachers to develop, maintain, and implement chemical hygiene plans based on OSHA's Laboratory Standard criteria (OSHA 29 CFR 1910.1450) and Right to Know Standard (OSHA 29 CFR 1910.1200).

- Support teachers of science by obtaining materials and resources from national, state, and local organizations that will inform and educate teachers about safe laboratory activities, safety procedures, and best practices in the teaching of laboratory-based science instruction.

- Review existing insurance policies to ensure adequate liability insurance coverage for laboratory-based science instruction.

- Provide teachers with sustained, comprehensive training in lab logistics—including setup, safety, management of materials and equipment, and assessment of student practices—at the time of initial assignment and before being assigned to a new exposure situation (OSHA 29 CFR 1910.1450[f][2]). This includes storage, use, and disposal of materials and chemicals; use of personal protective equipment; engineering controls; and proper administrative procedures. To ensure ongoing safety, annual training should be provided to keep teachers well informed about changes in safety procedures (NSTA 2000).

- Support the decisions of teachers to modify or alter activities in a safe manner or select safe alternative activities to perform in the science classroom/laboratory.

- Maintain adequately supplied, properly equipped, and safe facilities for performing lab instruction by conducting annual facilities audits (Motz et al. 2007; Ryan 2001).

To ensure a safe learning environment, members of the school board should:

- Recommend and support upgrading and improving school science facilities and science curriculum/instruction. If possible, a districtwide review of science facilities and instruction should be conducted at least every 3–5 years.

- Ensure that the district has adequate insurance to cover liability claims arising in the science classroom/laboratory.

- Adopt districtwide policies for safety, including guidelines for a safe working environment for all employees.

References

Anderson, E. R., J.S. Stanzler, and L.S. Masters. 1999. *Insurance coverage litigation*. 2nd ed. New York, NY: Aspen Law & Business Publishers.

Building Officials and Code Administrators (BOCA). 1996. Section 1008.0 Occupant Load (National Building Code).

Gerlovich, J.A., D. McElroy, R. Parsa, and B. Wazlaw. 2005. National school science safety indexing project: A beginning. *The Science Teacher* 72 (6): 43–45.

International Code Council (ICC). 2003. Section 15.1.7 and Table 1004.1.2 Occupant Load.

Motz, L.L., J.T. Biehle, and S.S. West. 2007. *NSTA guide to planning school science facilities*, Second Edition. Arlington, VA: NSTA Press.

National Fire Protection Association (NFPA). 2006. Section 10-1.7.0 Occupant Load, Life Safety Code 101–97.

National Research Council (NRC). 2006. *America's lab report: Investigations in high school science*. Washington, DC: National Academy Press.

National Science Teachers Association (NSTA). 2007. NSTA Position Statement: The Integral Role of Laboratory Investigations in Science Instruction.

National Science Teachers Association (NSTA). 2004. *Investigating safely; A guide for high school teachers*. Arlington, VA: NSTA Press.

National Science Teachers Association (NSTA). 2000. NSTA Position Statement: Safety and School Science Instruction.

Occupational Safety & Health Administration (OSHA). 1987. 29 CFR 1910.1200 Hazard Communication Standard (Right to Know Law).

Occupational Safety & Health Administration (OSHA). 1990. 29 CFR 1910.1450. The Laboratory Standard, Part Q (Chemical Hygiene Law).

Occupational Safety & Health Administration (OSHA). 1990. 29 CFR 1910.1450(f)(2). Occupational Exposure to Hazardous Chemicals in Laboratories.

Prosser, W.L., W.P. Keeton, D. B. Dobbs, R. E. Keeton, and D.G. Owen, eds. 1984. *Prosser and Keeton on torts*. 5th ed. Eagan, MN: West Group.

Roy, K. 2006. Proactive safety. *Science Scope* 30 (1): 72, 74.

Ryan, K. 2001. *Science classroom safety and the law: A handbook for teachers*. Batavia, IL: Flinn Scientific, Inc.

West, S.S., J.F. Westerlund, *A. L. Stephenson, and *N. Nelson. 2005. Conditions that affect secondary science safety: Results from 2001 Texas Survey, Overcrowding. *The Texas Science Teacher* 34 (1).

Additional Resources

Americans with Disabilities Act of 1990 (ADA). *See www.usdoj.gov/crt/ada/adahom1.htm and www.ada.gov/pubs/ada.htm*.

Building Officials and Code Administrators (BOCA). *See* www.iccsafe.org/help/redirect-bocai.html.

Individuals with Disabilities Education Act (IDEA). *See www.ed.gov/offices/OSERS/Policy/IDEA/index.html and www4.law.cornell.edu/uscode/20/1400.html*.

International Code Council (ICC). *See www.iccsafe.org*.

National Fire Protection Association (NFPA). *See www.nfpa.org*.

Occupational Safety & Health Administration (OSHA). U.S. Department of Labor. *See www.osha.gov*.

—Adopted by the NSTA Board of Directors
September 2007

Science Education for Middle Level Students

Introduction

NSTA recommends a strong emphasis on middle level science education, which can be achieved by staffing middle schools with teachers who are qualified to teach science and are trained and dedicated to working with students at this important period in their lives. Science concepts must be presented in an age-appropriate, engaging way so that students can build on their prior knowledge and attain the necessary background to participate successfully and responsibly in our highly scientific and technological society.

The middle school years, grades 5 through 9, are a time of tremendous physical, emotional, and cognitive changes for students. It *also* is a pivotal time in their understanding of and enthusiasm for science. Research has shown that if educators don't capture students' interest and enthusiasm in science by grade 7, students may never find their way back to science.

Declarations

NSTA recommends that teachers of middle level science

- Be fully qualified to teach science in their state and have a strong knowledge of science content.

- Attain a high level of knowledge about educational research on how middle level students learn, best practices, and effective instructional strategies for middle level students, and be able to use this knowledge in the classroom.

- Deal positively with the variability of behavior patterns of emerging adolescents.

- Support diverse learners effectively, deal with gender/equity issues, model a multidisciplinary approach to learning, and exhibit a desire to be a lifelong learner.

- Create a safe environment in which students can engage in inquiry-based science instruction in the classroom, in the laboratory, and in field settings described in the NSTA position statement Safety and School Science Instruction.

NSTA recommends that the curriculum of middle level science programs

- Be aligned with the science content and process skills outlined in the *National Science Education Standards*.

- Nurture curiosity about the natural world and include "hands-on, minds-on" inquiry-based science instruction.

- Engage students in laboratory investigations a minimum of 80 percent of the science instruction time as specified in the NSTA position statement Laboratory Science (*See www.nsta.org/about/positions/laboratory.aspx* and p. 137).

- Incorporate independent and cooperative group learning experiences during the study of science, and encourage informal learning experiences to support the curriculum.

- Integrate science with other curriculum subjects in a multidisciplinary approach, such as through theme-based learning.

NSTA recommends that the curriculum offer links to the real world by

- Applying content and skills learned in science class to students' own experiences.

- Connecting the classroom to the community through field trips, speakers, and local partnerships.

- Providing students with real-life experiences, such as mentoring and apprenticeships, that enable them to develop an awareness of science-based careers and an understanding of how science is relevant to their lives.

- Providing opportunities for decision-making activities (e.g., debate or research papers) and for involvement in community-based problems.

- Promoting societal goals for scientific and technological literacy.

NSTA recommends that the assessment strategies used in middle level science programs

- Include a variety of assessment methods that can be used to evaluate overall student achievement and guide decisions about instruction and practices.

- Be continuous and embedded in the instructional materials.

- Capture the interest of students to better engage them in the assessment process.

- Occur frequently to allow for modification, enrichment, and remediation. Include questions that are sensitive to gender and varied cultures.

NSTA recommends that middle level administrators support the science program by

- Providing numerous opportunities for professional development experiences to bolster teachers' knowledge of science content and enhance their skills in working with the middle level age group.

- Setting aside time for teachers to plan and strategize with colleagues in their own school as well as with those at the elementary and high school levels.

- Cultivating a dedicated team of teachers with a demonstrated expertise and interest in students in this age group, placing these teachers in the school system's middle schools, and permitting them to remain in their assignments so that they can develop their expertise.

- Supporting the recommended time allotted for middle level laboratory investigations.

- Providing necessary funding for laboratory investigations and science materials and resources.

References

National Research Council (NRC). 1996. *National Science Education Standards*. Washington, DC: National Academy Press.

National Science Teachers Association (NSTA). 2000. An NSTA position statement: Safety in the science classroom. Arlington, VA: NSTA.

National Science Teachers Association (NSTA). 1990. An NSTA position statement: Laboratory science. Arlington, VA: NSTA.

—Adopted by the NSTA Board of Directors
February 2003

Additional Resources

American Association for the Advancement of Science (AAAS) and National Science Teachers Association (NSTA). 2001. *Atlas of science literacy (Project 2061)*. Washington, DC: AAAS and NSTA.

Connecticut Science Supervisors Association. 1998. Science Teachers For the "Wonder Years" (The Critical Role of Middle School Science Teachers). (*www.cssaonline.net/cssawonderyears.html*)

Killion, J. 1997. What works in the middle: Results-based staff development. National Staff Development Council. (*www.nsdc.org/educatorindex.htm*)

Mizelle, N. B., Irvin, J. L. Transition from middle school into high school. Westerville, OH: National Middle School Association. (*www.nmsa.org*)

National Education Goals Panel Weekly Report. Turning Points 2000: A Look at Adolescence: November 30, 2000, Vol. 2, Number 81.

National Research Council (NRC). 2000. *Inquiry and the National Science Education Standards: A guide for teaching and learning*. Washington, DC: National Academy Press.

National Research Council (NRC). 2001. *Classroom assessment and the National Science Education Standards*. Washington, DC: National Academy Press.

National Science Teachers Association (NSTA). (2003). *Inquiring safely: A guide for middle school teachers*. Arlington, VA: NSTA.

National Science Teachers Association (NSTA). (1998). *NSTA Pathways to the science standards (middle)*. Rakow, S.J., editor. Arlington, VA: NSTA.

Responsible Use of Live Animals and Dissection in the Science Classroom

Introduction

NSTA supports the decision of science teachers and their school or school district to integrate live animals and dissection in the K–12 classroom. Student interaction with organisms is one of the most effective methods of achieving many of the goals outlined in the National Science Education Standards (NSES). To this end, NSTA encourages educators and school officials to make informed decisions about the integration of animals in the science curriculum. NSTA opposes regulations or legislation that would eliminate an educator's decision-making role regarding dissection or would deny students the opportunity to learn through actual animal dissection.

NSTA encourages districts to ensure that animals are properly cared for and treated humanely, responsibly, and ethically. Ultimately, decisions to incorporate organisms in the classroom should balance the ethical and responsible care of animals with their educational value.

While this position statement is primarily focused on vertebrate animals, NSTA recognizes the importance of following similar ethical practices for all living organisms.

Including Live Animals in the Classroom

NSTA supports including live animals as part of instruction in the K–12 science classroom because observing and working with animals firsthand can spark students' interest in science as well as a general respect for life while reinforcing key concepts as outlined in the NSES.

NSTA recommends that teachers

- Educate themselves about the safe and responsible use of animals in the classroom. Teachers should *Seek* information from reputable sources and familiarize themselves with laws and regulations in their state.

- Become knowledgeable about the acquisition and care of animals appropriate to the species under study so that both students and the animals stay safe and healthy during all activities.

- Follow local, state, and national laws, policies, and regulations when live organisms, particularly native species, are included in the classroom.

- Integrate live animals into the science program based on sound curriculum and pedagogical decisions.

- Develop activities that promote observation and comparison skills that instill in students an appreciation for the value of life and the importance of caring for animals responsibly.

- Instruct students on safety precautions for handling live organisms and establish a plan for addressing such issues as allergies and fear of animals.

- Develop and implement a plan for future care or disposition of animals at the conclusion of the study as well as during school breaks and summer vacations.

- Espouse the importance of not conducting experimental procedures on animals if such procedures are likely to cause pain, induce nutritional deficiencies, or expose animals to parasites, hazardous/toxic chemicals, or radiation.

- Shelter animals when the classroom is being cleaned with chemical cleaners, sprayed with pesticides, and during other times when potentially harmful chemicals are being used.

- Refrain from releasing animals into a non-indigenous environment.

Dissection

NSTA supports each teacher's decision to use animal dissection activities that help students

- develop skills of observation and comparison,

- discover the shared and unique structures and processes of specific organisms, and

- develop a greater appreciation for the complexity of life.

It is essential that teachers establish specific and clear learning goals that enable them to appropriately plan and supervise the activities. Teachers, especially those at the primary level, should be especially cognizant of students' ages and maturity levels when deciding whether to use animal dissection.

NSTA encourages teachers to be sensitive to students' views regarding dissection, and to be aware of students' beliefs and their right to make an informed decision about their participation. Should a teacher feel that an alternative to dissection would be a better option for a student or group of students, it is important that the teacher select a meaningful alternative.

Finally, NSTA calls for more research to determine the effectiveness of animal dissection activities and alternatives and the extent to which these activities should be integrated into the science curriculum.

Regarding the use of dissection activities in school classrooms, NSTA recommends that science teachers

- Conduct laboratory and dissection activities with consideration and appreciation for the organism.

- Plan laboratory and dissection activities that are appropriate to the maturity level of the students.

- Use prepared specimens purchased from a reputable and reliable scientific supply company. An acceptable alternative source for fresh specimens (i.e., squid, chicken wings) would be an FDA-inspected facility such as a butcher shop, fish market, or supermarket. The use of salvaged specimens does not reflect safe practice.

- Conduct laboratory and dissection activities in a clean and organized work space with care and laboratory precision.

- Conduct dissections in an appropriate physical environment with the proper ventilation, lighting, furniture, and equipment, including hot water and soap for cleanup.

- Use personal safety protective equipment, such as gloves, chemical splash goggles, and aprons, all of which should be available and used by students, teachers, and visitors to the classroom.

- Address such issues as allergies and squeamishness about dealing with animal specimens.

- Ensure that the specimens are handled and disposed of properly.

- Ensure that sharp instruments, such as scissors, scalpels, and other tools, are used safely and appropriately.

- Base laboratory and dissection activities on carefully planned curriculum objectives.

- Be prepared to present an alternative to dissection to students whose views or beliefs make this activity uncomfortable and difficult for them.

—Adopted by the NSTA Board of Directors
June 2005

References

National Research Council (NRC). 1996. *National Science Education Standards*. Washington, DC: National Academy Press.

Additional Resources

Cross, Tina R. 2004. Scalpel or mouse: A statistical comparison of real and virtual frog dissections. *The American Biology Teacher*, 66(6): 408–411.

Institute of Laboratory Animal Resources, Commission on Life Sciences, National Research Council, National Academy of Sciences, National Academy of Engineering. 1989. Principles and Guidelines for the Use of Animals in Precollege Education. *dels. nas.edu/ilar/prin_guide.asp*.

Kinzie, M. B., R. Strauss, and J. Foss. 1993. The effects of an interactive dissection simulation on the performance and achievement of high school students. *Journal of Research in Science Teaching* 30(8): 989–1000.

Kwan, T., and J. Texley. National Science Teachers Association. 2002. *Exploring safely: A guide for elementary teachers*. Arlington, VA: NSTA Press.

Kwan, T., and J. Texley. National Science Teachers Association. 2003. *Inquiring safely: A guide for middle school teachers*. Arlington, VA: NSTA Press.

Madrazo, G. 2002. The debate over dissection: Dissecting a classroom dilemma. *The Science Educator* (NSELA). EJ64162.

NSTA POSITION STATEMENTS

National Science Teachers Association (NSTA). 2000. Safety and School Science Instruction, an NSTA Position Statement. *www.nsta.org/about/positions/safety.aspx*.

Texley, J., T. Kwan, and J. Summers. National Science Teachers Association. 2004. *Investigating safely: A guide for high school teachers*. Arlington, VA: NSTA Press.

The Integral Role of Laboratory Investigations in Science Instruction

Introduction

A hallmark of science is that it generates theories and laws that must be consistent with observations. Much of the evidence from these observations is collected during laboratory investigations. A school laboratory investigation (*also* referred to as a lab) is defined as an experience in the laboratory, classroom, or the field that provides students with opportunities to interact directly with natural phenomena or with data collected by others using tools, materials, data collection techniques, and models (NRC 2006, p. 3). Throughout the process, students should have opportunities to design investigations, engage in scientific reasoning, manipulate equipment, record data, analyze results, and discuss their findings. These skills and knowledge, fostered by laboratory investigations, are an important part of inquiry—the process of asking questions and conducting experiments as a way to understand the natural world (NSTA 2004). While reading about science, using computer simulations, and observing teacher demonstrations may be valuable, they are not a substitute for laboratory investigations by students (NRC 2006, p. 3).

For science to be taught properly and effectively, labs must be an integral part of the science curriculum. The National Science Teachers Association (NSTA) recommends that all preK–16 teachers of science provide instruction with a priority on making observations and gathering evidence, much of which students experience in the lab or the field, to help students develop a deep understanding of the science content, as well as an understanding of the nature of science, the attitudes of science, and the skills of scientific reasoning (NRC 2006, p. 127). Furthermore, NSTA is committed to ensuring that all students—including students with academic, remedial, or physical needs; gifted and talented students; and English language learners—have the opportunity to participate in laboratory investigations in a safe environment.

Declarations

NSTA strongly believes that developmentally appropriate laboratory investigations are essential for students of all ages and ability levels. They should not be a rote exercise in which students are merely following directions, as though they were reading a cookbook, nor should they be a superfluous afterthought that is only tangentially related to the instructional sequence of content. Properly designed laboratory investigations should:

- have a definite purpose that is communicated clearly to students;

- focus on the processes of science as a way to convey content;

- incorporate ongoing student reflection and discussion; and

- enable students to develop safe and conscientious lab habits and procedures (NRC 2006, p. 101–102).

Integration of Labs into the Science Program

Inquiry-based laboratory investigations at every level should be at the core of the science program and should be woven into every lesson and concept strand. As students move through the grades, the level of complexity of laboratory investigations should increase. In addition, NSTA recommends that teachers and administrators follow these guidelines for each grade level:

Preschool and Elementary Level

With the expectation of science instruction every day, all students at the preschool and elementary level should receive multiple opportunities every week to explore science labs that fit the definition described in the Introduction.

Laboratory investigations should provide all students with continuous opportunities to explore familiar phenomena and materials. At developmentally appropriate levels, they should investigate appropriate questions, analyze the results of laboratory investigations, debate what the evidence means, construct an understanding of science concepts, and apply these concepts to the world around them.

Middle and High School Levels

With the expectation of science instruction every day, all middle level students should have multiple opportunities every week to explore science labs as defined in the Introduction. At the high school level, all students should be in the science lab or field, collecting data every week while exploring science labs.

Laboratory investigations in the middle and high school classroom should help all students develop a growing understanding of the complexity and ambiguity of empirical work, as well as the skills to calibrate and troubleshoot equipment used to make observations. Learners should understand measurement error; and have the skills to aggregate, interpret, and present the resulting data (NRC 2006, p. 77).

As students progress through middle and high school, they should improve their ability to collaborate effectively with others in carrying out complex tasks, share the work of the task, assume different roles at different times, and contribute and respond to ideas.

College Level

At the college level, all students should have opportunities to experience inquiry-based science laboratory investigations as defined in the Introduction. All introductory courses should include labs as an integral part of the science curriculum. Laboratory experiences should help students learn to work independently and collaboratively, incorporate and critique the published work of others in their communications, use scientific reasoning and appropriate laboratory techniques to define and solve problems, and draw and evaluate conclusions based on quantitative evidence. Labs should correlate closely with lectures and not be separate activities. Exposure to rigorous, inquiry-based labs at the college level *also* is important because most teachers develop their laboratory teaching techniques based on their own college coursework laboratory experiences.

Support for Teachers of Science

To give teachers at all levels the support they need to guide laboratory investigations as an integral part of the total curriculum, NSTA recommends:

- Ongoing professional development opportunities to ensure that teachers of science have practical experiences that familiarize them with the pedagogical techniques needed to facilitate inquiry-based labs matched to appropriate science content (NSTA 2006, NRC 2006, p. 150–151).

- Yearly evaluation of the laboratory investigations to determine if they continue to be an integral and effective part of the whole program and the delivery of all content.

- Periodic training in lab logistics, including setup, safety, management of materials and equipment, and assessment of student practices. Safety equipment and annual safety training should be provided so that science educators are well informed about yearly changes in safety procedures to ensure that students and educators are protected (NSTA 2000).

- Training to work with students with academic or remedial needs, physical needs, and gifted and talented students so that teachers can differentiate instruction appropriately. Assistive equipment, additional personnel, and facilities, modified as needed, *also* should be provided to ensure appropriate instruction of all students.

- Effective preservice programs that prepare teachers to carry out science labs as a central part of every science curriculum.

Support for Science Labs

To ensure that laboratory investigations are implemented in schools, administrative support is crucial. NSTA recommends that the school administration recognize the instructional importance, overarching goals, and essential activities of laboratory investigations and provide the following:

- An adequate facility where labs can be conducted. At the preschool and elementary levels, this means a classroom with sufficient work space, including flat moveable desks or tables and chairs, equipment, and access to water and electricity. At the middle and high school levels, a safe, well-equipped lab space should be available, with necessary equipment and access to water and electricity. In addition, appropriate facilities to work with students with special needs should be provided. (Biehle et al. 1999)

- Adequate storage space for all materials, including devices and materials in common use that are considered hazardous. (Biehle et al. 1999)

- Funding for yearly educator training on how to manage materials and guide inquiry-based learning during labs.

- A budget for regular maintenance of facilities and equipment, as well as annual costs for new or replacement equipment, supplies, and proper waste management.

- A budget that recognizes additional costs required for field experiences.
- Laboratory occupancy load limits (number of occupants allowed in the laboratory) set at a safe level based on building and fire safety codes, size and design of the laboratory teaching facility, chemical/physical/biological hazards, and the needs of the students (Roy 2006; NSTA 2000). Science classes should have no more than 24 students even if the occupancy load limit might accommodate more (NSTA 2004). Research data shows that accidents rise dramatically as class enrollments exceed this level (West et al. 2001). Teachers should not be faced with a Hobson's choice—teach in an unsafe environment or sacrifice the quality of teaching by not doing labs.

Assessment

Assessment, a powerful tool in science education, serves both formative and summative purposes. Not only does it help show what students have learned and the nature of their reasoning, it *also* indicates what gaps remain in learning and what concepts must be reviewed (NSTA 2001). NSTA recommends the following steps to ensure that laboratory investigations are part of the assessment process:

- Teachers of science, supported by the administration, be given the time and training to develop assessments that reveal and measure inquiry skills—the ability to design, conduct, analyze, and complete an investigation, reason scientifically, and communicate through science notebooks and lab reports.
- Instruction and assessment be aligned so that formative and summative assessments are meaningful and can be used to improve the science curriculum as well as determine what students have learned.

—Adopted by the NSTA Board of Directors
February 2007

References

Biehle, J. T, L. L. Motz, and S. S. West. 1999. *NSTA guide to school science facilities*. Arlington, VA: NSTA Press.

National Research Council (NRC). 2006. *America's lab report: Investigations in high school science*. Washington, DC: National Academy Press.

National Science Teachers Association (NSTA). 2006. NSTA Position Statement: Professional Development in Science Instruction.

National Science Teachers Association (NSTA). 2004. NSTA Position Statement: Scientific Inquiry.

National Science Teachers Association (NSTA). 2004. *Investigating safely: A guide for high school teachers*. Arlington, VA: NSTA Press.

National Science Teachers Association (NSTA). 2001. NSTA Position Statement: Assessment.

National Science Teachers Association (NSTA). 2000. NSTA Position Statement: Safety and School Science Instruction.

Roy, K. 2006. (Lack of) safety in numbers? *Science Scope* 30(2): 62–64.

West, S.S., J.F. Westerlund, N.C. Nelson, and A.L. Stephenson. 2001. Conditions that affect safety in the science classroom: Results from a statewide safety survey. Austin, TX: Texas Association of Curriculum Development.

Additional Resources

Clough, M.P. 2002. *Using the Laboratory to Enhance Student Learning. Learning Science and the Science of Learning,* ed. R. W. Bybee, 85–96. Arlington, VA: NSTA Press.

Learning Conditions for High School Science

Preamble

Science educators face many challenges—including national standards, state standards, district goals, and public demands—as they attempt to provide safe and effective science learning. Science students and educators require adequate working conditions to meet these challenges.

Rationale

Science students deserve a safe, effective learning environment. This requires safe and adequate conditions, adequate facilities and equipment, and competent, qualified teachers.

Declarations

The National Science Teachers Association recommends the following standards for creating and maintaining science learning conditions:

- Science teachers should be certified in the science they are teaching
- New teachers should be assigned master science teachers as mentors
- Science teaching assignments should provide time for preparations necessary for safe and effective science teaching
- Science teachers should be scheduled in only one classroom to be able to manage the laboratory safely
- Science students should learn in classrooms that have the facilities and space for a safe laboratory-oriented program
- Students need adequate space to work safely. Because of safety considerations and the individual attention needed by students in laboratories, science classes should be limited to 24 students
- Science rooms/laboratories should be used only for science classes and science activities and should be equipped with:
  - Adequate laboratory space per student and sufficient gas, electrical, and water outlets for student laboratory activities
  - Safety equipment, such as fire extinguisher, fume hoods, emergency showers, and eyewash stations
  - Audiovisual equipment such as an overhead projector; videocassette recorder and monitor; slide projector; and one or more computers with internet access, plus needed software and maintenance service
  - Sufficient storage for equipment and supplies and preparation space close to the classroom

- Support equipment such as photocopying machines, typewriters, word processors, and telephone in a nearby and accessible area

- Textbooks for each student, laboratory guides, and references as appropriate and needed

• Science teachers responsible for classes with special education students in an inclusion setting need

- Special education support adequate to safely and successfully meet the individual education plan of each inclusion student in the science classroom

- Access to professional development in teaching in an inclusion classroom

- Additional planning time with the special education teacher assigned to her or his classroom to modify the learning environment to better facilitate the safe learning process for those students with special needs

- Additional resources, professional development, and equipment and materials provided as necessary for inclusion students to be safely and completely involved in the least restricted science learning and activities.

References

Kochhar, C. A., and L.L. West. 1996. *Handbook for successful inclusion*. Gaithersburg, MD: Aspen Publishers.

National Research Council (NRC). 1996. *National Science Education Standards*. Professional Development Standard A, Teaching Standard D, Program Standard D, Program Standard F, and System Standard D. Washington, DC: National Academy Press.

New Jersey Department of Education. 2000. Planning is key to success in Howell Township. *Inclusion Insights*. (spring). Trenton, NJ: New Jersey Department of Education.

U.S. Department of Education (U.S. DoE). 2000. Before it's too late: A report to the nation from the National Commission on Mathematics and Science Teaching for the 21st century, GOAL 3: Improve the working environment and make the teaching profession more attractive for K-12 mathematics and science teachers. Washington, DC: U.S. DoE

Authors

NSTA Committee on High School Science Teaching, Anne Tweed, Director (1999–2001), Beverly Nelson, Director (2001–2004)

—Adopted by the Board of Directors
July 1986; Revised February 2002

▽ RESOURCES

Online

American Chemical Society—*www.acs.org*

Animals in the classroom

- Montgomery County Public Schools Regulation: *www.mcps.k12.md.us/departments/policy/pdf/ecjrb/pdf*
- National Association of Biology Teachers: *www.nabt.org/sub/position_statements/animals.asp*
- Institute for Laboratory Animal Research: *http://dels.nas.edu/ilar_n/ilarhome/index.shtml*

Chemical database (searchable)—*chemfinder.camsoft.com*

Chemical hygiene plan (writing a)—*www.osha.gov/SLTC/laboratories/index.html*

Chemical management information—*www.instantref.com/tox-chem.htm*

Flinn Scientific Company—*www.flinnsci.com/Sections/Safety/safety.asp*

National Fire Protection Association—*www.nfpa.org*

Centers for Disease Control and Prevention (CDC)—*www.cdc.gov/od/ohs/Ergonomics/labergo.htm*

Centers for Disease Control and Prevention (CDC)

- Lyme disease—*www.cdc.gov/ncidod/dvbid/lyme/index.htm*
- Bloodborne pathogens—*www.cdc.gov/niosh/topics/bbp*
- Hepatitis—*www.cdc.gov/ncidod/diseases/hepatitis/index.htm*

Heating safety (video clips about) Journal of Chemical Education Chemistry Comes Alive! *http://144.92.39.64/JCESoft/CCA/CCA0/C6/C6101000101.html*

Laboratory Dissection (Regents Prep)—*http://regentsprep.org/regents/biology/units/laboratory/dissection.cfm*

Laser pointers (Safety recommendations for use of)   *www.rli.com/resources/pointer.asp*

- Vanderbilt University laser safety manual—*http://frontweb.vuse.vanderbilt.edu/vuse_web/facstaff/VUSE_Laser_Safety.pdf*

Model rocketry (Connecticut Code)—*www.state.ct.us/dps/DFEBS/OSFM/regs/modrock.pdf*

National Association of Rocketry—*www.nar.org*

National Fire Protection Agency Code for Model Rocketry—*http://nfpa.org/aboutthecodes/AboutTheCodes.asp?DocNum=1122*

National Institutes of Health (NIH)—*http://odp.od.nih.gov/whpp/ergonomics/laboratory.html*

Occupational Safety and Health Administration (OSHA) at *www.osha.gov.*

- Bloodborne Pathogen Standards—*www.osha.gov/SLTC/bloodbornepathogens/standards.html*

Oklahoma State University Environmental Health and Safety—*www.pp.okstate.edu/ehs/links/labchem.htm*

RECOURCES

Poisonous plants

- Cornell University—*www.ansci.cornell.edu/plants/alphalist.html*
- University of Pennsylvania—*cal.nbc.upenn.edu/poison*
- Botanical.com—*www.botanical.com/botanical/mgmh/poison.html*
- Poisonous Plants and Animals—*library.thinkquest.org/C007974/intro.htm?tqskip1=1 &tqtime=1204*
- Yahoo Directory—*dir.yahoo.com/Science/Biology/Botany?Plants/Poisonous_Plants*
- Colorado State University—*www.vth.colostate.edu/poisonous_plants*

Special needs (Teaching science to students with)—*www.as.wvu.edu/~scidis*

Team teaching (Some notes on) —*www.wiu.edu/users/mfsam1/TeamTchg.html*

U.S. Environmental Protection Agency (EPA)—*www.epa.gov.*

- EPA Region 7 Lab Science Safety Equipment Requirements for Middle Schools— *www.epa.gov/region7/education_resources/teachers/ehsstudy/ehs14.htm*

Print

Kwan, T., and J. Texley. 2002. *Inquiring safely: A guide for middle school teachers.* Arlington, VA: NSTA.

Martin, R. 1994. What the courts have said about inclusion. *LDA/Newsbriefs* May/June: 22–25.

National Research Council (NRC). 1996. *National Science Education Standards.* Washington, DC: National Academy Press.

Osborne, A.G., and P. Dimattia. 1994. The IDEA's least restrictive environment mandate: Legal implications. *Exceptional Children* 61: 6–14.

Ryan, K. 2001. *Science classroom safety and the law: A handbook for teachers.* Batavia, IL: Flinn Scientific.

▽ INDEX